Signs, Cosigns & Off On Tangents

Signs, Cosigns & Off On Tangents

Olivia Taylor-Young

charett press

ISBN: 0-7392-0416-5

Library of Congress Catalog Card Number: 99-96624

Charett Press, Brentwood, California 94513

Signs, Cosigns & Off On Tangents

Published 1999. First Edition
Printed in the United States of America
06 05 04 03 02 01 00 6 5 4 3 2

Taylor-Young, Olivia
Signs, cosigns & off on tangents

1. Taylor-Young, Olivia 2. Essays 3. Opinion 4. Social commentary

This book has been set in 10.5/13.5 New Century Schoolbook. Accents are set in Helvetica.

MORRIS PUBLISHING
3212 East Highway 30 • Kearney, NE 68847 • 1-800-650-7888

Contents

II
Personal, Political and Miscellaneous Dilemmas

Preface

Signs, Cosigns & Off On Tangents has nothing to do trigonometry… a disclosure which should get me off the hook for questionable spelling. 'Signs' are the signs of our times. 'Cosigns' are the social interactions they cause and 'Off On Tangents' refers to the wide range of subjects these commentaries cover.

Since this range also covers some well-established ground, I wrote the following hoping to reflect the German poet Goethe's words, "The most original modern authors are not so because they advance what is new, but simply because they know how to put what they have to say as if it had never been said before." But if 'never' is too strong an ideal, I'll settle for challenging status quos… such as pop culture's quest for absolutes and easy answers.

In that case, I submit that there are no categorical certainties in human relationships. At the same time, I realize that all theories, including my own, are subjective… so I've made it a critical point to examine related topics from many angles. The chapters "Children of the Heart" and "Toss the Laundry List Into the Garbage" for example, empathize with parents whose grown children have become alienated or chosen to self destruct; and both take issue with the culture of blame that renders parents responsible for all the ills of the world. On the other hand, "Ritual Torture" determines that when home and family are not havens—but covens of cruelty—no one is obligated to remain devoted to abusive relatives. It is even OK to boycott a mother's funeral.

I've also tried to demonstrate that issues rarely happen in a vacuum. "Oh, Yes You Do!" describes malicious people who turn words into weapons. "Easter Week" depicts word weaponry on the professional level, dealing with malice in the media. And in summation, "Evil Has Many Allies" cites the consequences of denying the existence of malice or covering it up or remaining neutral in the face of it.

These—and all the chapters in *Signs, Cosigns & Off On Tangents*—vary greatly from one another; yet they are bound together by some surprisingly common principles, themes and human qualities. And while some of its subjects are intentionally painful and disturbing, I've also tried never to lose sight of humor as the great healer. I want my readers to identify, analyze, feel, experience, understand and even cry... but not jump from a seventh-story window.

Above all, my goal was—and is—not to get readers to think the way I do, but to give them food for thought. Which begs the question of why, since I'm no alleged expert, should anyone care about what I think, think about what I write... or give a damn about my goals or intentions. Well, I guess I'm a true child of my generation... I've never outgrown believing that one person can make a difference. I also agree with the premise "the people who make a difference are not the ones with the credentials, but the ones with the concern."[1] So, while I've culled together a few credentials in my lifetime, given the choice, I favor concern.

I also vote for experience. I am a wife, ex-wife, mother, stepmother, grandmother, career woman, daughter, sister, friend and observer of humankind. I've lived through the pain and aftermath of divorce and the joy of a twenty-year (at this writing) marriage to my most beloved friend. Having raised a family, I have known great happiness and tragedy as profound as burying my youngest child. In the working world, I've had on-the-job success; yet have also endured sexism, discrimination and Dilbert-like dopiness. Across the years, I have undergone many personal changes and witnessed even more in the world at large... and come to the conclusion that all of life's experiences are simply a microcosm. A mirror of the human condition.

Recently, when I read some excerpts from *Signs...* to a church group, someone asked me where I'd studied insight. A grinning son of mine quickly replied, "She got it from her kids." While not entirely true, neither was his response inaccurate. My children and step-children have given me experiences and views of the world that I could never have imagined otherwise. And as an author, I see, feel, absorb, and reflect upon what I encounter and observe, and respond with the written word. Perhaps this is where I find my 'insight.' Most certainly, it is my truest credential to turn my thoughts into *Signs, Cosigns & Off On Tangents.*

One more thing about credentials. They can be highly overrated and, in fact, I know how easily one can be dubbed an expert. When my first book, *The Child Snatchers*[2], was published in 1982, few people seemed interested in or were doing much about missing children... which is the reason why my co-author and I wrote it in the first place. In short order: I was a media resource, a talk show guest, an expert witness and a consultant for attorneys, law enforcement and the Legislature. During that period, when I once called Senator Alan Cranston's office about the status of a bill, I was told they had no information; however, they could give me the name of a local expert. To my astonishment, they referred me... to me!

I learned from that experience never to take myself—or any expert—too seriously. Years later, I'd long refocused my career into healthcare public relations; and on the day of my youngest son's tragic death, an emergency room staffer handed me a brochure and suggested I read it because it contained "expert advice" on grief. I handed it back. I had written it.

That encounter powerfully reinforced what I'd give anything not to know firsthand. Theory is theory and life is life... and often one has little to do with the other. Which is not to say I discount all expertise. Many of my chapters are extensively footnoted because I freely quote those whose eloquence I wish I'd thought of and whose ideas help strengthen my case. Conversely, where I believe popular sentiment or authoritative opinions are misleading and even dangerous, I say so... because the vast, underrepresented population caught between 'expert' theories and life's realities is especially my reading public. They are the reason this book was written. And *Signs, Cosigns & Off On Tangents* is dedicated to them.

Them... and my husband, Kirk Taylor, whose love, support

and unfailing encouragement truly made this book possible. Not only is he my best friend, he is my live and live-in grammar- and spell-checker, thesaurus, critiquer and infinitely patent marshaller of my thoughts. 'Greater love hath no man... ' than he who sittith in bed at 6:00 o'clock on a workday morning lovingly editing the umteenth revision of his wife's manuscript.

—Olivia Taylor-Young
Brentwood, California
May 1999

✍

1. And the Angels Were Silent / Max Lucado

2. The Child Snatchers / Bobbi Lawrence and Olivia Taylor-Young (Charles River Books, 1982)

Acknowledgments

Many people have generously shared their time, insights and personal experiences to help make *Signs, Cosigns and Off On Tangents* a reality. In fact, every supporting anecdote or recollection in this book either stems from my own experience or was related to me by others. In deference to everyone's privacy, however, and because of the often sensitive nature of personal stories, I have taken the liberty of deleting some names, changing others and compositing a few minor details. Yet even where I've sheltered my sources, or relied on hearsay or someone else's memory, I have tried to narrate each example as accurately and truthfully as possible.

Some relatives, friends and acquaintances may be surprised to see themselves reflected in print. Others were enthusiastic contributors. But whether they were amenable or unknowing, I am deeply grateful and indebted to all whose examples I drew from. Because we crossed paths, they have added strength to my ideas, helped to solidify my viewpoints and provided me with inspiration, perspective and balance. Occasionally, even negative balance. Finally, there are some very special people who deserve special mention and have my abiding love.

To my son Bob, whose love and support has been my constant in an inconstant world; to Bobbi Lawrence and Phyllis Gordon, my sisters of the heart, whose love, insights, editorial comments and unfailing support have sustained me through just about everything; to Gail Griffin for her thoughtful perspectives… and for keeping me motivated; to Lorene Lederer who so generously shared her friendship, editorial skills and artistic talents; to my friends and family who've been so enthusiastic and complimentary when they've read my manuscripts; and, one more time, to my loving and beloved husband, I owe a debt of gratitude I can never repay and can only say 'thank you' time and time again.

I

Relating to Home and Family—Including Household Pests

Children of the Heart

The Opposite Side of Child Abuse

He was six that September, an inquisitive blue-eyed dynamo with scraped knees and sun bleached hair. He loved to learn and already knew how to read. "I spelled banana today," the boy proudly told his Grandpa. "But I didn't know when to stop."

She was also six, a brown eyed charmer with auburn curls... and more comfortable in overalls than the green velvet pinafore she wore that day. The little girl seemed enthralled seeing *The Nutcracker* for the first time. Her mommy glowed with pride, thinking, "My daughter loves ballet." Until the child complained loudly, "I've been listening and listening and can't hear a word!"

There was another little girl whose voice rang loud and clear. In a museum filled with viewers, her mortified Daddy tried to shush her as she pointed to paintings of cherubs and exclaimed, "That's a boy baby! See, he's got a penis just like my little brother. And that one's got a penis and that one... "

They played. They pondered. Misstepped, misspelled and mispronounced. They discovered, delighted and sometimes embarrassed us with their views of the world. Yesterday's children. Where are they now?

At nineteen, he was an addict with a history of suicide attempts. His latest psychiatrists were uncertain if the youngster who'd once spelled banana was truly schizophrenic or if his apparent schizophrenia was drug induced. "These patients often know something is wrong with them," one doctor explained. "They take the drugs to mask the symptoms. We call it self medication."

The girl who couldn't hear ballet self medicated, too. At fourteen, she was drinking with friends. At eighteen, she joined (and quit) AA for the first time. At twenty-six, seven months pregnant with her third child, she OD'd on crack and her five-year-old son discovered his mommy's near lifeless body. Her own once glowing—now grieving—mother would recall the younger woman's vows she'd not even take an aspirin without consulting the obstetrician. As it was, the baby, delivered by emergency cesarean, died as she was born—in pain and too soon.

The sun-bleached speller survived, if one can call it that. Doctor after doctor stressed his only alternative was, 'acknowledge your illness and own your addiction. Then commit to treatment and, even more important, to getting well... or as well as possible.' But denying such illness is a prevalent and powerful symptom. Likewise is repeating patterns and blaming others. So he turned his back on one treatment center after another and the ensuing years saw progressive deterioration join forces with irrational rage and resentment. His family tried unconditional love. Understanding. Compassion. Counseling. "If you were standing between him and his drugs," a therapist told his mother, "he'd mow you down without a second thought." Those who loved him most eventually came to fear him. And to realize their connections had become co-dependency in an addictive relationship. Finally, they had to say 'enough.' They no longer see him. No longer know his address... if he has one. Tragedy happens.

It happens again and again, with variations to the theme. The parents of the once tiny patron of the arts despaired over her chronic refusal to accept responsibility for her actions. "I failed the exam because the teacher is stupid," at age twelve. "My checks keep bouncing because the bank makes mistakes," at twenty. She lied to her family, her teachers, her friends and herself. And when she got caught, she'd cry and play hapless victim. Her parents took comfort in the knowledge some perfectly horrible adolescents grow into perfectly fine adults. They gave her every benefit of the doubt and afforded her every opportunity. They also tried unconditional love, understanding, compassion, counseling and, eventually, 'Tough Love.' In turn, she blamed them for her every shortcoming and told anyone who'd listen that she was a victim of whatever abuse the imagination could conjure up.

Had her lies not been contradictory as well as outrageous, this young woman could have put her entire family at risk. Instead, she merely caused excruciating pain. Similarly afflicted families often do not fare as well, however. Many are torn asunder by false perceptions, condemnation and the need to safeguard a distorted agenda.

Some losses are forced upon us. Others are the result of pain-filled choice. Yet while grief can spring from varied sources, it manifests itself the same. In the decade since that family's petulant daughter quit school and moved in with someone who turned out to never hold a job, her every self destructive decision, derailed career move and failed relationship—including two unhappy marriages—has been either her mother's and/or father's 'fault.' At first, both parents were bewildered, hurt—even defensive—and incapable of believing she'd carried such infantile patterns into adulthood. Then, they became justifiably angry. Finally, as resigned acceptance replaced heartbreak and outrage, they drew strength from refusing to pay the price of ongoing abuse in order to keep the relationship alive. No longer did they allow their daughter to denounce them or lay blame. No longer did they try making sense of her blatant lies. They also declined all requests for money, although it meant not hearing from her otherwise.

This had never been an abused or neglected child. None of these children were. Each had been well cared and well provided for. All had social and educational opportunities. Love was the natural ingredient in their parents' feelings toward them; and never in the worst trials and error of family life had there been an intent to make them suffer. All of this notwithstanding, each developed a history of feeling hostile, dissatisfied and out of place.

On the other hand, were the mothers and fathers of these children—and others like them—perfect? Of course not. Were they widowed or divorced? Some were, some weren't. Did they do the best with the resources and information they had? Most likely most of the time. And did they make mistakes? Absolutely... and probably lots of them because they were human. Still are, as a matter of fact. Parents who may lie awake during torturous nights asking, *What happened to the child I loved so? Where have we failed? What could I have done differently...* until they eventually learn through their grief that such questions are moot because, in all likelihood, their answer is *nothing.*

Parents are conduits who bring their children to life; however, the chosen destination of any person's life-path belongs to him or her alone. That reality—acknowledging how little control one actually has over a growing or grown child's destiny—may give parents a helpless feeling; yet, it is also a healthy letting go. Moms and Dads provide the outer trappings, protection and guidance during the early years. But, just as the doctor told the young man he had to own his addiction, so must people growing into adulthood accept responsibility for the content and consequences of their character.

Why then are some children—even from the same family—able to overcome all of life's odds while others seem destined to fail and/or fall apart at the slightest provocation? Why do some achieve and/or meet the world head on while others remain too terrified to try? Why do some youngsters grow into loving, productive adults while others become amoral, anti-social and/or otherwise disgusting? These questions have been asked throughout the ages, and their answers both vary with the times and remain the purest of speculation. How much is genetic? How much is environmental? Would that there was a simple solution to the complexities of humankind. What comfort it would bring to countless families of the alienated, and to every parent who ever had to commit a beloved adolescent or adult son or daughter to an addiction clinic, a mental hospital... or a grave.

But this is not about speculating *what if* or *why.* It is about *when.* What happens when parents try love, understanding, reaching out, substituting compassion for anger, *ad infinitum,* and still get kicked in the face? What happens when an adult child refuses contact because of long-held grudges or misperceptions? Or claims that family ties will cause collisions with a UFO? What happens when grown children play cruel, passive-aggressive games and/or resort to threats and extortion? Perhaps these mothers and fathers can join or become founders of support groups named things like *Parents of Abusive Adults,* or *Parents of People-Born-Too-Emotionally-Fragile-to-Make-It-in-an-Imperfect-World,* or *Parents of Adult Children of Whatever-Dysfunction-is-Currently-in-Vogue.* Perhaps, if they are lucky, they can take comfort from other children who are doing OK. But can they reconcile the ongoing sense of loss? A sense that the natural order of things has been brutally interrupted and ties between generations have been truncated in such an ugly manner?

And what about family folklore? Those verbal Kodak moments that should be preserved and passed on to the grand-kids. Moments like our watching TV's annual Spring showing of *The Ten Commandments* the year my youngest son was seven. As the Angel of Death advanced through Egypt, the little boy looked at me, then warily at his oldest brother, then back at me again and pronounced, "Thanks Mom for not making me the first born." I always hoped to share that story with his kids, for such anecdotes create the bridge between a family's past and future. But what if there is no future? For us, the last born tragically became the first gone... and when he died at twenty-eight, he left not only a hole in our hearts, but no children with whom to share his legacy.

Yet death is not the only kidnapper of part of a family's future. Parents do not expect to bury their children. But neither do they expect to lose them in other ways. To the thrall of addiction. The lure of a cult. The darkness of mental illness beyond reach. Or to the unthinkable choice between accepting a grown child's abuse or having him/her disappear from their lives in a morass of outrage, false accusation and hatred.

How do parents come to terms with these types of losses? How do they cope with a loved one's denunciation, detachment or downright self destruction? With what amounts to personal betrayal or feels like wasted years? With the reality of grandchildren that not only may never be, but—as grandparents—they may never know about or see? Or hold in their arms and share the family's stories?

For the most part, they experience devastation, shock and a whole range of conflicting emotions. They touch the depths of human pain and reveal, to their own astonishment, the breadth of their strength. Faced with harsh, unimaginable reality and the option of open-ended grief, instead they come to respect their separateness, redefine new boundaries and accept that "There is a wholeness about the person... brave enough to let go of his unrealistic dreams and not feel like a failure for doing so... "[1]

They also come to understand that, while hope is important because it makes everything easier to bear, unreasoning hope can blind one to reality and blindside the future... so they learn to face reality and make peace with what is. Some illnesses are simply not curable. Some damages, irreparable. Counsel to *never give up* or tales of the prodigal son notwithstanding, sometimes the fate of Humpty Dumpty is more authentic. Things can go too far. Or repeat themselves once too often... and even unconditional love has to stop short of emotional suicide.

"She was the light of my life," recalls the alienated daughter's father. "But so much has happened that a fantasyland reunion where everyone just forgives and forgets won't—can't—work. We'd be nuts if we didn't wonder what she really wants or if it's worth more pain to find out." After a long pause, he adds, "Sure, bygones are supposed to be bygones, but there's no way around it—you can't have a relationship without trust."

Reality can be excruciating. Yet by coming to terms with it and embracing the present in spite of personal tragedy, these parents allow themselves to do more than survive. They learn to go forward... because, cliché as it sounds, life does go on. And so, too, can precious memories.

A father remembers the light of his life. And the mother of the boy who spelled banana notes, "Of course I pray *maybe someday.* But I've long since stopped blaming myself, waiting for the phone to ring or feeling guilty about enjoying my life." Thoughtfully, she adds, "For a long while I couldn't look at small children. The pain was too great—thinking what could happen, or what could have been. Then, out of the blue, it struck me what an adorable child he really had been and no one, not even the man my son had become, could take those memories away from me."

And so he became a 'child of the heart.' A child grown older without growing up. A child who spread wings... then seemed to disappear into unexplained, unreachable darkness. A child whose precious memory serves not as a bridge between the past and the future, but as a coping mechanism for those who loved him.

The road to adulthood is often bumpy and filled with unexpected obstacles. 'Children of the Heart' are those who, for any number of reasons, get lost along the way. In the mind's eye of the mothers, fathers, siblings and other loved ones who wait in vain for them at the finish line, they remain locked in childhood... because the present is too painful and there seems no viable continuation to their story.

✍

1. How Good Do We Have To Be? Rabbi Harold S. Kushner (Little Brown & Co. 1996)

Ritual Torture

The Rite Thing is Not Necessarily the Right Thing

The woman hung up the phone, aware she felt absolutely nothing. No grief. She'd done her grieving years ago. No relief. The news would have negligible impact on her day-to-day existence. No regret. She knew beyond a shadow of a doubt her decision to sever ties had been both appropriate and necessary. "The opposite of love truly is indifference," she sighed, then went to tell her husband and children that her mother had died.

They had not seen the deceased in nearly ten years. Still, the only sorrow the mother's passing evoked was for those she had hurt during her lifetime. The question then became one of funerals. Is a decision to avoid them ever justified? Ever socially acceptable? Acceptable to whom? Was history and/or reality altered by the woman's death? "She made *Mommie Dearest* look like *Mary Poppins,*" the daughter finally concluded. "Half a century of abuse was enough. I can't be a hypocrite and I think I'd throw up if I had to listen to eulogies."

Husband, children and dearest friends, all who would have been by the woman's side had she opted to attend the mother's burial rites, felt greatly relieved at her determination to stay away. They also applauded the strength of character which allowed her to stick by that decision.

Sometimes what appears to be the right thing is absolutely wrong. Not going to a parent's funeral has all the earmarks of flagrant insensitivity and moral blindness. So does not rushing to the bedside of those who are dying. But neither the facts nor the pain of having been grossly abused are automatically erased because the perpetrator reaches old age or falls victim to a life-limiting illness.

Among the basic principles of caring for the terminally ill are: *Never judge the family dynamics and do not attempt to "make right" a lifetime of what has gone wrong.* These precepts are an integral part of training for every hospice worker and volunteer. A nurse with whom I team-taught classes on death and dying stressed those points as among the most important our students could ever learn. Then, she ruefully shared her own experience of having decided to break the rules.

One of her first hospice patients was a man with terminal cancer whose three grown daughters refused any contact. His wife—mother of the daughters—repeatedly begged the nurse to intervene. "Please speak with them," she'd plead. "Tell them all is forgiven. Make them understand how important it would be for us if only they'd come."

Against her better judgment, yet feeling so sorry for the parents, the nurse approached the daughters. They rebuffed her in no uncertain terms. The father had raped all three for many years during their childhood, she was told. And, yes, Mommy was aware of it. She had, in fact, cautioned them the family would starve if anyone told and it would all be the little girls' faults. In later years, the mother brushed aside any confrontation with "It was so long ago what does it matter?"

Only through extensive therapy, strong support for one another and breaking ties with their parents had these adult daughters begun to heal. Were they wrong not to rush to Daddy now? Would they have been expected to play the deathbed scene with any other child molester or rapist? The effects of evil often outlive its perpetrator. It was a lesson the well-meaning hospice nurse never forgot.

The incident taught her other things as well. Some relationships are defined within a very narrow context and that is exactly where they should remain. Her job was to provide loving care to her patient. She continued to do so with consummate skill; nevertheless, as a human being, she was burdened with information she wished she did not have.

She also realized that, unless one is privy to all the details, conclusions about absent offspring or relatives can come from a faulty major premise. Access to details however, is really irrelevant. Personal decisions remain the business only of the people who must make them. By the way, these daughters did not attend the funeral either.

Rituals mark every one of life's occasions. Within families—and the more numerous the progeny the more frequent the events—there are always baptisms or bar-mitzvahs or burials to attend, with graduations and weddings and assorted holidays thrown in for good measure. This can be wonderful in a loving, warm, supportive family, or even one where things are only fairly pleasant or mildly tolerable. Whether happy or sad, occasions become a time of reunion. A time for those scattered far and wide to come together and celebrate the very fact they are related.

But what if family connections are nothing to celebrate? If being in the company of one's relatives means mingling with people who clearly cannot stand you, or one another? What if family members are emotionally and/or physically violent? Or just being around them for whatever reason gives a person the willies or sends someone into weeks of anxiety and depression? What if attending a certain event will impose severe financial hardship? It is essential then to realize rituals are not more important than the individuals involved. Neither First Communion nor wedding ceremonies were created to make guests unable to buy groceries. The season of 'Peace on Earth' does not mean one has to put him/herself in the middle of a war zone.

Yet avoiding holiday conflagrations is among our population's most difficult choices... making holiday seasons for therapists akin to the tax season for accountants. Clients storm the barricades for last-minute and/or emergency counseling. Hot-line phones ring off the hook. Whether in anticipation or post mortem, people are overwhelmed with guilt, fear, disillusion and indecision. To the professionals however, solutions to some of these problems can be cut and dried.

A successful businessman, married and the father of three, sought counseling on how to survive 'going home' for Thanksgiving. Over the years, he'd tried ignoring, accepting and even reasoning with his own super-critical father. He'd also confronted the older man about his relentless attacks... to no avail. Every visit, get-together and special occasion precipitated the son being subjected to verbal degradation and abuse. Now, he wanted to know how he could get through the day without his stomach tying up in knots. "The question isn't how can you get through dinner," the therapist made a helpless gesture with her hands. "The question is *why* do you want to go?"

The option to actually stay away had never occurred to the client. "We're family!" he protested. "My children need their grandparents." "Oh really?" the therapist replied. "Does 'family' mean being treated like trash? Does it mean children witnessing their own father being undermined and degraded? Are you certain they are immune from the same abuse? Scrap your illusions. Let's get real."

What does 'getting real' involve? Mikal Gilmore, author of *Shot in the Heart,* theorizes, "...the most dangerous unexamined belief we have is that the family is the microcosm of an ideal world." Chronicling his own family's violent history to determine what turned his brother, Gary, into a killer, Gilmore came to feel "...I don't think my family was quite the aberration people would like to believe. I think we were a hidden norm."

Whether or not they were actually a norm, the concept of hidden is a common family denominator. People are often bound by what they believe is convention or what they imagine is true for everyone's family but theirs. Like children, they may feel guiltily responsible for any failure in a family; so they invent or try recreating ties which never truly existed. They pretend everything is like a Norman Rockwell Thanksgiving when a more accurate family portrait may be an empty room or some famous battle scene. And they continue the façade year after year because admitting the truth seems more painful than living the lie.

There is a terrible price for masking reality, often paid in terms of failed physical and emotional well-being. But there is a price for unmasking the truth as well... because a stinging sub-consequence of familial abuse is other relatives' need to cover it up. So those who refuse to perpetuate a family's pretense, no matter how heinous the behavior, often incur everyone else's wrath.

Angry relatives may be driven by their own need for fabrication, their own inability to handle the pain. They may sincerely feel keeping quiet is in everyone's best interest or that they can stay out of the fray and remain neutral. However, to the 'whistle-blower' the dynamic translates to: What happened to you is inconsequential—even if it includes rape or other assorted atrocities—what is important is the appearance presented to the outside world.

A person who tacitly approves of violence by pretending it does not exist cannot truly wish the victim well. Does one really wish to break holiday bread with people like that or see them dancing at a daughter's wedding? Staying away then, becomes a viable, intelligent option. It also turns into an ironic decision. Even though the person making it may simply have had enough and wishes only to be left alone, his/her absence translates to a glaring presence among those who prefer to gloss over the truth.

The violence need not be as dramatic as rape. Emotional abuse, such as what the businessman faced with his father, hardly comprises a day at the beach. Families strangle themselves over issues of control; yet, power struggles over the soul of a twenty-five-... or forty-... or sixty-year-old... border on absolute insanity. Treating adults as eternal children has no place in a viable family. Neither have grudges mired in childhood misperceptions. Survivors of true violence are hardly in the same category as an ex-kid who was ordered to clean up his/her room. Mommy/daddy and sibling relationships must yield to adult respect and *vice versa*. And, if they do not, there is no law against people creating their own traditions.

No statute condemns young couples to day-long trips in heavy traffic in the company of restless toddlers, only to be ridiculed when they arrive at their destination. No law requires people to host hostile relatives who bash and destroy. If getting together with blood relations means subjecting oneself, one's spouse and/or one's children to battling, belittling or just an overall bummer, going through the motions simply makes no sense.

There is also no decree which says holidays cannot be enjoyed in the company of those who truly love or like one another, even if the bonding is through caring, not chromosomes. It is the same with all ceremonies and rituals. Choosing who not to invite to a momentous occasion is the prerogative of its central characters. It is the graduate's day. The baptized baby's parents' day. The bride and groom's day. Where violence or cruelty are concerned, people have the right to keep occasions free from those who would spoil them. Likewise, not attending something like a niece's wedding may have nothing to do with loving the happy couple. If the aunt and/or uncle in *absentia* would suffer personal anguish in the presence of their enemies, the newlyweds will be just as married without them.

As will a couple whose parents decline to bankroll a bridal extravaganza. Nowhere has the idea of family ties and rituals become more distorted than when lovers say "I do." To the wedding industry, 'tradition' means big bucks... to be spent by the bride's parents. Often, it means the same to the happy couple. But elaborate weddings are a gift, not an entitlement. A license to marry is not a license to extort. The bride who expects Mom and Daddy to foot the bill for a sumptuous ceremony and reception is not a 'victim' if her parents feel a modest celebration is more realistic or appropriate. Or if they feel the couple themselves should assume some costs. Any bride and groom who cannot underwrite the festivities, yet are outraged at Mom or Dad for not making them the greatest show on earth, are not mature enough to be marrying in the first place.

Rituals are human-made. Their form can be human-reinvented. There is a great freedom in knowing it is appropriate to say 'no.' In learning how to enjoy holidays and special occasions among people who truly care. In the ability to take certain family 'obligations' with a grain of salt rather than a bottle of Maalox. This encompasses the right to boycott festivities, to leave people off the guest list and to choose whether or not to foot the bill. Most of all, it means freedom from the double life of hypocrisy.

Victor Hugo once said, "To live a life which is a perpetual falsehood is to suffer unknown tortures." He was right. Pretending for the sake of image, in the name of family and/or because one is afraid to deal with the truth, is like an addiction. It condemns one to a life of fabrication and those who are mired in it suffer as much from covering up as from fear of exposure. When bloodlines mean brutal bondage, when it is more important to protect an abuser than acknowledge the victim, than loosening—even severing—family ties means breathing fresh, free air. It really is OK to *Just Say No!*

✍

Faerie Tales, Myths and Happily Ever After

Yes! You Can Find Classified Love!

It is a great, technolovable story. A formerly-married woman living in northern New England powers up her computer and connects with a formerly-married guy from the Pacific Northwest. Letters, phone calls and cross-country visits follow. And the minister who performs their wedding ceremony not only prays, but paraphrases... that remarriage is the triumph of hope over experience.

Will this couple live happily ever after? Who can tell? I only know that my husband and I wish them the best, considering their faerie tale romance seems like a cyberspace equivalent of our own.

A long time ago in what seems like a kingdom far away, I was a divorced mother raising three sons. Things were different back then. In today's world of virtual reality, one-parent families are acknowledged, if not always fairly or favorably. In the decades where social morés reflected the leftover myth of fifties' television, however, single parents allegedly did not exist.

Perhaps that myth was a by-product of post-World War II yearnings for domestic tranquillity. Perhaps it was fabricated to bolster the post-war consumer society. In any event, early TV families portrayed a world where no one remained single, everyone lived happily ever after, all households were economically stable and no family experienced dysfunction of any kind. Nobody was ever hit by cancer or a drunk driver either. Not only was divorce an aberration, there was also no such thing as being widowed at twenty-nine.

As long as sponsors could depend upon selling the stuff of domestic utopia, this fiction prevailed... and familial television altered only slightly over the years. By the seventies, for example, single parents could be acknowledged as long as they (1) were 'cured' and (2) had a housekeeper to help with all the kids. But no Brady boy ever sneered "you're not my real mother" at Carol, Cindy wasn't in therapy, and step-dad Mike was never downsized or—fairly or unfairly—accused of abuse.

Since it was woven from the fabric of untruth, however, the myth unraveled eventually, along with many marriages. In spite of TV role models, suddenly there was a whole new underclass: single parents with children to support in a country without adequate child care. Moms from middle-class backgrounds applied for welfare because child support orders were a joke. Formerly- and/or never-married women struggled daily against opportunity and salary discrimination in the workplace, and single parents of both sexes jeopardized their jobs every time a family emergency occurred.

Legends die hard. Little—if any—correlation was made between defective relationships and the rising divorce rate. Even less attention was paid to remarriages ending in equally high numbers, or to evidence that the unwed are happier and in better health than those locked into disastrous unions. Instead, the societal response was—and still is in many cases—to dismiss the unmarried as inherently flawed and to view any form of being single as an unnatural, temporary event to be remedied as quickly as possible.

"You wouldn't have to worry your pretty little head about such things if you had a husband," a Family Service Director pooh-poohed my responsibility to support three children. He then suggested that I flit from job to job to look for eligible men. The widowed fared little better. Scant attention was given to the reality of grief, time to heal and the memory of the person who had passed away. On the day her thirty-year-old husband died of cancer, a friend was 'consoled,' "Don't worry, you'll be married again within a year."

Yet despite a culture which denied our existence, life continued to happen for 'we the discoupled.' We went back to school, set out on career paths, took care of our families and helped fashion new attitudes and laws on everything from equal pay to child custody to welfare reform. Whether single by chance or choice however, most of us agreed there is more to existence than the fight for survival and parity. And whether or not marriage was in one's karma—or eventual life plan—most adults desire the closeness, intimacy, sharing and companionship that accompanies a good romance.

That was easier said than done. I recall longing for good morning cuddles from someone over the age of eight. I also recall numerous discussions with fellow singles about the limited opportunities to 'meet someone' beyond the high school or college campus. Aside from the impracticality of job surfing, workplace romances can be risky for obvious reasons. And, in spite of themselves, people are more likely to learn something in adult education courses rather than finding potential dates. Singles' clubs, dances, discussion groups and bars often toss unweds together with nothing more in common than their marital status. For the non-hitched however, that scene often looked like the best alternative.

It also meant braving the unknown. Nineteenth-century pioneers headed by covered wagon to conquer America's frontier. Feeling every bit like pioneers, we, their latter-day single counterparts, traveled by public transportation or late model car to prospect in uncharted societal territories. Both sets of circumstances were ripe for disappointment. The wide-open, old-West, for example, attracted greedy speculators caring nothing for the rights of others. Similar things could be said about the singles' scene. There had to be another way. A reasonable method of making contact which was safe, uncontrived, humiliation-free, did away with dehumanizing backdrops of competing chatter and clinking glasses, and allowed for intelligible and even intelligent conversations.

When the idea of personal ads first surfaced, it carried the same type of stigma as trying to sell a sexually transmitted disease. Only the farthest out alternative newspapers would publish romance-seeking personals and the ads themselves usually sought something more kinky than a plain old meaningful relationship.

Two decades later, classified dating is no longer in the closet. Judiciously giving them such labels as 'A Great Way to Meet People,' mainstream newspapers offer "Personals" on multiple pages of multiple choice. And, while some ads may still raise a few eyebrows, the majority simply translate to *nice person would like to meet someone similar.* There are columns for the 'Golden Years': *Slender, sensuous seventies plus seeks senior of substance.* There are categories for men wanting to meet women and vice versa. There are also columns for men wanting to meet men and women, women... which proves that, as a nation, we are growing up, and more than thirty years after Bob Dylan first said so, the times really are 'a-changin.'

Then again, are they? The "Personals" remain on a par with unmarried sex in the nineteen-fifties: lots of people participate, but few are willing to admit it. Those who do 'own up' often confess in furtive whispers or claim they glimpse at classifieds only for laughs rather than to meet a partner.

Who can blame them? Even though singles can meet unsavory characters at church or through well-meaning, unwitting friends, fiction based on homicidal maniacs perusing the columns hits the best seller list. Likewise, TV talk shows treat 'Classified' and 'On Line' couples as they are revealers of a dirty secret... and even sic a stable of alleged experts on them to justify the derision.

In another bit of irony, publications which offer on-line services often disparage chat rooms and one-on-one contact via cyberspace. Newspapers which publish personal ads also print articles about their potential danger and/or chide them as listings of losers. Of course discretion and safety precautions are an absolute must. But what a paradox. In a society where single is synonymous with temporary and where unwed is euphemistically referred to as an alternative lifestyle, whenever the unattached take steps to become attached, they are ridiculed by the peek-a-boo press.

Much of this journalistic voyeurism occurs because juicy innuendo sells. Yet I wonder how many who report it also go home to the loneliness of an empty apartment. Perhaps they ought to log onto the Internet. Or try the personals. Yes, oh horror! That is how I met my husband back in 1978. And while this shocking revelation may cause microscopic inspection of our psyches by so-called experts, it comes as no surprise to family, friends and just about anyone who has known us longer than ten minutes.

At the time, I was collaborating on my first book and juggling part-time jobs to keep the roof over my family's head. Submerged in research, writing, editing and rewriting—with spare recreational moments reserved for the children—all social life virtually had ceased.

It was the same for my co-author. Eventually however, both of us got fed up with our cloistered existence. I recall discussing the pros and cons of our trying the personals, and finally deciding *why not?* Since it was barely a socially acceptable thing to do in those days, I believe we, both career women well past adolescence, also swore one another to secrecy.

Yet furtive or not, the classifieds appeared to be a convenient, cost-effective way to expand our social horizons... with additional advantages of comfort, safety and anonymity. The presumption was, and still is, correct. One advertisement has the potential of netting a dozen or more answers and its placement price is far below the total outlay for gas, parking, baby sitters, new outfits and buying dinner or drinks. Conversely, if one wishes to be reactive instead of pro, at most, it costs a phone call or one stamp for each reply.

Putting thoughts on paper and mailing a letter also eases the stress of that initial getting-to-know-you ritual. Similar kudos are now given about putting thoughts on a screen and sending them into cyberspace. People usually reply to an ad through a P.O. or newspaper box number. As with on-line ventures, this means respondents are free to reveal only as much personal information as they wish, including a home address and/or place of work. In both instances, one then has the opportunity to eliminate the weird sounding, impersonal or otherwise unsuitable before following up on the intriguing. And both sender and recipient can become acquainted within the security of home. Lounging around in a robe or at least not having to get dressed up, they also have the option of hanging up should they suspect their pen-or-cyber pal is a fraud, or if the encounter becomes boring or obnoxious. By the time the parties decide to chance meeting face to face, they have at least reduced the risks of needing to extricate themselves from a less-than-desirable blind date.

There are no guarantees any of this will result in a lifetime commitment or even one pleasant evening. But considering all the positives, it was a formula worthy of consideration in 1978... and remains so today.

Like all love stories, ours has its own unique twist. Back when I was weighing the pros and cons of a 'personals' adventure, my future husband was a divorced, custodial father raising daughters ages eleven and nine. Turned off by the singles' scene, yet not adverse to the idea of a good romance or an occasional interesting date, the classifieds made sense to him as well. However, it was my co-author's ad which caught his attention.

Several days after her classified ran in the *San Francisco Bay Guardian,* an envelope full of replies arrived during one of our editing sessions. Instead of a coffee break, we took an answer break, marveling like kids on Christmas as thirty-seven responses tumbled out of what we jokingly called 'the plain brown wrapper.'

One letter was a sensitive, open, honest self-evaluation, filled with gentle humor. I thought it was the best of the lot. The writer even claimed a particular weakness of mine, salt and pepper hair. Overwhelmed by sheer volume, my collaborator handed me that letter insisting thirty-six others were enough to choose from. Besides, she observed 'Old Salt and Pepper' and I seemed perfectly matched. How prophetic those words. Yet at the time, I faced the problem of tactfully explaining to a prospective date why he had been passed from friend to friend like an old shoe. There was no way to disguise myself as the true advertiser either. People give their ages when responding to the personals and both the original letter writer and 'Old Salt and Pepper' were five-and-one-half years my junior.

I pondered my approach. Did I really want to do this? Did I really even want to call a man who was younger than me? It took from Tuesday until the following Sunday to make up my mind. Finally, I decided to phone him and open the conversation by saying "You answered an ad, but it wasn't mine." "I love it," he laughed. And thus began a week in which, although a dinner date was planned for Friday, we logged over thirty hours of toll-call conversation and threw ourselves into Ma Bell's debt for months to come.

We also irreversibly bound ourselves into one another's hearts. Before we ever met face to face, we understood each other's views on religion, politics, feminism, astrology, our children, our parents, our careers, our pasts, our hopes for the future, our visions for the world. We had traveled vastly different roads of life experience, yet now found one another at near identical junctions. We tested each other, seeking sets of values and searching for meanings in questions and reply. It was important to know how much looks really mattered on a scale of one to ten. "Suppose I told you I weigh three-hundred pounds?" I challenged. "Depends on how tall you are," he replied. He also broke the social taboo and initiated discussion of our sexuality. "If our horoscopes are correct," he said with hesitation, "we probably ought to wear chastity belts Friday night." To which I shot back, "Why don't we just skip dinner?"

Three weeks from the dinner we did *not* skip, we became engaged. Three weeks after that, we were married. Neither one of us recommends such a whirlwind courtship for every couple and both suppose we'd have had heart attacks had our kids followed suit; yet we honestly believe we were soul mates who got lucky. It has not, however, always been happily ever after. In fact, my former clergyman's once shameful brush-off of, "don't worry, some day you'll remarry and all your troubles will be over," is our in-house joke. Troubles and challenges do not evaporate with the words, 'I do.' They are inherent in the normal ups and downs and wonders of living. We blended two families, endured split loyalties and outlasted the adolescence of three teenagers born within eighteen months of one another. We have sustained each other through tragedy, job loss, career changes and life-threatening illness on more than one occasion. We have also known incredible joy. Through the life we have built together, the experiences we've known and, most important of all, what we enduringly share as best friends, lifetime companions and devoted lovers.

Not every personals' romance turns out this way. And not every cyberspace encounter can endure real reality. But some do. I only know that all these years later we still marvel at having found one another, sing the praises of how we met and remain strong classified ad-vocates. We also have a message for sociologists, writers and curious TV talk show hosts: put away your microscopes, pens and microphones. Allow single people of any persuasion to live and meet in privacy... and in peace. Few people still marry the kid next door. Those who do often find themselves dating again in their thirties, forties, fifties and beyond. Spare them your stereotypes and, frankly, mind your own business. Instead, wish for them—and for yourselves as well—the happiness which can be found in this brave new world. Even in a classified ad.

✍

It Ain't the Brady Bunch

*Sabotaged Step-Parents—-
And the Kids Who Do Them In*

The phrase 'blended family' always reminds me of frozen orange juice. Blend, after all, is synonymous with reconstitute. Another synonym for blend is step. Step... as in spouse's child of a previous marriage or the not-biological parent married to one's mom or dad. Whatever the word, when it comes to reconstituting a family, reconstruction may provide a more accurate description. Reconstruction... as in post-Civil War, when hope ran headlong into never-ending obstacles and often turned into disaster.

Step-families face innumerable challenges. They are also an enigma. Can a step-parent legally sign a report card? Access academic or medical records? Authorize a child's treatment in case of an illness or accident? If a child is hospitalized and visitors are limited to immediate family, does this include: the step-mother married to the custodial father? The step-father married to the mother with custody? Both step-parents married to parents who share custody and/or the non-custodial parent (and step-parent)?

For the most part, the answers vary with individual circumstance and the questions remain a focal point of countless discussion groups. One such group, a seminar, entitled *Blended Families—Legal and Ethical Dilemmas for Healthcare Providers,* was sponsored by the pediatric unit of a hospital where I was Director of Public Relations.

I sat in on the conference planning sessions along with a committee of highly skilled professionals. Format and content fell easily into place; yet, not until a nurse-panelist burst into tears and told us, "I wish my only worry was authorization to treat...", did we truly zero-in on sum and substance.

Two years ago, the panelist went on to explain, she'd married a widower with children ages seven and ten. "Now, the kids act like I'm responsible for their mother being dead and I feel like I don't have permission to exist." Struggling to regain her composure, she added, "I absolutely hate going home."

"I only see my step-kids on weekends," another nurse responded. "That's more than enough. I've ended up with asthma attacks from their outright rejection... and, hey, I wanted to love them, too!"

Noting that the primary cause of step-family divorces are children from the previous marriage, the committee's legal advisor added that his wife sided with her teen-age daughters when they taunted, "You're not my father. You and your rules can go to hell." Nodding in agreement, a social worker confided she was going through a divorce because her husband refused to believe his children were capable of bad—or even mischievous—behavior; consequently, the kids underwent a personality change the moment he walked out the door. They threw things at their step-mother. Called her names. Hit, kicked and scratched her. 'Daddy' then accused her of self-inflicting the bruises and/or lying about the origin.

We never really got back to planning the seminar that day. Instead, it became a time of sharing, empathy and support. Professional expertise aside, everyone there had either experienced step-parenthood first hand or was close to someone who had. All of us conceded not every step-parent is a good one. In fact, some are horrible and frightening. We also agreed that pain, grief, sense of loss and split loyalties are valid problems which need to be addressed; and, in a step or *any* type of family, children must be protected from abuse. However, the crux of that day's conversation was victimization turned the other way around and the consensus was clear. An astounding amount of abuse in blended families emanates from the children.

Respected child raising expert Dr. T. Berry Brazelton cautions step-remarrieds not to expect appreciation from their spouse's children. Most who've been there tend to agree. Apparently in youngster's eyes, step-parents are viewed as pretenders to the throne and/or seducers of Mom or Dad's affection. Feeling replaced as well as conflicted, these children are generally less than overjoyed about entering a new family situation and cling to their past like a life raft... even if the past was not so hot. They may also secretly hope for reconciliation against all odds... and perhaps even a magical resurrection. In any case, love is the last thing they want to feel for or accept from the perceived usurper.

On the other hand, in spite of Brazelton-type warning labels and the awesome responsibility of raising someone else's children, step-parents often do not understand the enormity of what lies ahead. Neither do they equate lack of appreciation with potential rage, acting out and even sabotage. Instead, they marry with blinders on, believing the societal fairy tale that if they give the youngsters enough love and time, the kids will learn to love 'em in return. And everyone will benefit from their brand new life.

It happens. But it also happens that trauma is inherent in the definition of 'step.' After all, without previous trauma, there would be no present step-family... and no one is immune to traumatic fallout. No matter how devoted any step-parent may be, he/she is a constant reminder to the child of the Mom or Daddy who is no longer there. And whether that parent has died, disappeared or simply no longer shares the same address, and unmindful of how long ago the event took place, a resentful step-child just *knows* it was the step-parent's fault.

A woman marrying a widower may be disliked or even hated for no other reason than she is alive and the child(ren)'s mother is not. Kids visiting a weekend Daddy are often outraged at having to share his attention. Wanting his wife to vaporize—or to vaporize his wife—they behave accordingly. Spouses of custodial mothers and fathers are expected to share in the care, support and running of a household where, as parents, they are neither welcome nor respected... and are often mistreated. They are also supposed to offer unconditional love to—and be willingly responsible for the welfare of—non-blood related children who openly hate their guts.

With maturity, children come to understand a parent's death was not voluntary nor was the deceased likely to have been particularly overjoyed at the prospect. Younger children, however, draw little comfort from such knowledge. Feeling willfully abandoned, those with a parent who has died carry emotional burdens similar to children whose fathers or mothers have selfishly opted to eschew all responsibilities. Reactions to true or perceived abandonment run the gamut from vilifying *"I hate her for leaving me..."* to excuses *"She really loves me, but ...."* to children holding themselves personally responsible *"If I'd been a good boy, Daddy wouldn't have gone away..."* Yet two reactions do appear consistent: (1) The remaining parent eventually gets the blame. If I'd been good transforms into *"If she/he'd been better, this wouldn't have happened..."* And (2) let a step-parent enter the picture and, no matter what or how youngsters really feel, they begin to worship and even deify Mom and/or Dad in absentia.

According to theory, children who refuse to accept a step-parent carry a hurt so deep they simply cannot respond. Another theory says fear of being abandoned again drives them to punish the step-parent in advance and act out a scenario of 'get him before he gets me.' Still another says some kids are simply rotten brats. Whatever the reason and whatever the circumstance, that children are capable of cruelty is nothing new; but what they do to one another on the playground is truly child's play compared to what they are capable of doing to their mother's husband or father's wife. Verbal and physical abuse is commonplace. And since a child's imagination can run wild when attached to a vendetta, so is telling anything from tall tales to vicious slander. Knowing the youngster is acting out pain or simply putting on an act is too often small consolation for any step-parent forced to defend his/her sanity and self against devastating accusations. Patience and understanding have their limits.

Besides, it is one thing to be lied about and quite another to have the falsehoods believed. Especially if the person who gives unquestioning credence to the lies is the partner one has chosen for life. Of prime importance then, in parent-child-step-parent relationships, is fortification of the husband-wife relationship. So, too, is reinforcing the structure of a family's organizational chart. Husband and wife are supposed to be the primary unit. One which remains a viable, united entity as children come and grow and go. This concept is no less valid for step-families but, since they start out upside down with the kids preceding the couple, it does not always work.

One reason things fall short is that remarried parents frequently carry needless, overwhelming guilt. Having failed to shield their children from some of life's most unpleasant realities, the widowed are filled with contrition (although powerless to have altered the fact) and the divorced feel guilty whether or not the idea was theirs or the split-decision was justified, absolutely necessary and right. Unfortunately, guilt without foundation often blinds a parent to his or her progeny's human frailty.

Never has a child been born who won't test a new situation to its utmost. The best of youngsters search for loopholes in any limits and, if they find even the tiniest one, will drive a truck through it. No situation could be more ripe for the testing than a newly blended family. The children have fears, worries, misdirected anger and the need to define their place. They also instinctively sense insecurity in the adult(s) upon whom they depend. A child's needs must be considered; yet, so must the parents. And so must the fact that love between husband and wife does not preclude the love between parent and child, it is simply different. Mothers or fathers who tell their children *you are loved completely, but John—or Mary—is my lifetime partner* are not being cruel. They are setting the boundaries, and hopefully the stage, for a successful family unit.

On the other hand, parents who are neither willing nor able to stand by their partner are doing their children no favor. By believing an angelic face is incapable of wrongdoing, they are teaching their kids to substitute 'being cute' for having a conscience. By dismissing a spouse with clichés such as *blood is thicker than water,* or blindly insisting 'my kids come first regardless of circumstance,' they are actually handing their youngsters the power to decide the fate of a family.

Among the consequences of such empowerment are: children who grow up resentful because they were burdened with calling the shots; children who wallow in a sense of demanding entitlement and do not grow up at all; or children who grow up as masters of deceit and/or shackled by guilt... especially if they succeeded in tormenting or getting rid of a step-parent. P.S. Those very same youngsters will also, a few years down the road, be gibing at mom or daddy to 'get a life.' After all, they, the kids, are entitled to lives of their own.

So how do we sum up blended families? At any given time, we can have: angry, displaced-feeling youngsters; parents who cannot handle the reality of their disobedient, hurting children; step-parents who feel emotionally battered by the kids and abandoned by their partners; and husbands and wives who are mutually disillusioned by their spouse's apparent betrayal. Combine any of the above and you have a recipe for disaster. As an added ingredient, there may even be an 'ex' (or two) who limits parent/child contact to gift giving and trips to the amusement park, thus dumping both custodial and step-parents into the roles of ogre against the never-ending-giver-of-good-times. All in all, the step-parent doesn't stand a chance.

Often, neither does the marriage. Relationships cannot survive when one partner's existence is resented and his/her integrity cast in doubt. Marriages cannot survive continuous upheaval, especially when one or both partners feel betrayed. But blended families can and do survive... and by the very same guidelines which apply to all families: problems can be overcome if (1) they are faced with honesty and (2) underlying good will exists on all sides. Hope lies in every member's willingness to take whatever steps are necessary to preserve both individual self esteem and the sanctity of the family. Neither can be sacrificed for the other.

Dysfunction is not synonymous with the existence of problems. People without problems are either imaginary or dead. However, if problems are confronted by shooting the messengers who expose them, that is when dysfunctions flourish and families disintegrate. If a child's goal is to break up a parent's marriage, if kids insist a parent choose between them and his/her spouse, if they consider a step-parent a temporary inconvenience to be disposed of as quickly as possible, then one way or another—succeed or fail—the family must come to terms with all of this.

Success and failure are relative. Which word, for instance, pertains to the social worker's taking leave of her untenable family situation? Is she a success for facing up to a painful truth or a failure for not accepting more abuse in the name of trying even harder to make things work? And how does the succeed-fail concept apply in deciding where, with whom and by what rules a child will live?

Many families confuse success with making the impossible possible. Just as they mistakenly link a youngster's motives with parental merit. For silly (from an adult's view) or sensible reasons, a child may genuinely want to live with the other parent. If there doesn't seem to be a hidden agenda, and all else is relatively equal, perhaps the switch is worth a try. On the other hand, if a kid thinks of the change as a way to run amok, or is attempting to bludgeon the custodial parent and/or make him/her dump a step-parent, then maybe the youngster should also get his or her way. For better or worse—and possibly God help the other parent—but the child might learn about consequences and/or taking responsibility for one's own actions.

Or perhaps not. Nevertheless, there still may be an upside... peace could descend upon the blended household. After a teenage step-child left to live with the non-custodial parent, one woman confided to her family's therapist, "I thought we would grieve... but instead we feel nothing but relief." "I'd worry if you did grieve," the counselor replied. "The kid was brutalizing you." Perhaps from guilt, or perhaps because it seemed like the right thing to say, the woman protested, "But it's our child!" To which the therapist shot back, "Every ax-murderer is somebody's child!"

Behind even the most charming, angelic face may lurk the soul of a brat. Parenthood—single or remarried status notwithstanding—does not compel one to overlook that fact. Nor does it oblige one to sanction a child's present-day tantrums because of yesterday's traumas. Becoming a mom, dad or either step-gender is not synonymous with surrender of one's human needs, feelings and rights. Children need to get that message. They also need to get the messages that remarriages count, and families are meant to be headed by adults; not the kid's ideal of, today I can rule the household—and tomorrow the world—by tyranny. For starters, the rest of the world is not going to be so accommodating.

None of us can guarantee our progeny a perfect world. At the same time, regardless of past pain and disappointment, life is always full of fresh hope and opportunity. That is another message children need to get; for it is precisely what a new marriage represents... the chance to begin again. It is the parents' place to take hold of the reins and allow themselves that chance. It is the children's place to accept and honor that. And to respect the threshold and integrity of the home and bedroom shared by their parent and step-parent. That is the only way a blended family is going to work.

To Everything There is a Season

The Misguided Myth of the Empty Nest

To everything there is a season,
and a time to every purpose under heaven.
—Ecclesiastes III

His skin was indescribably soft, his tiny face, exquisite... and his diminutive fingers had a grip equal to the jaws of life. Overwhelmed with love, I held my firstborn child and vowed to always keep him safe from harm.

Fast forward three-plus decades. Month-old twins lay kicking the air and cooing. "What do I do to protect them?" their mommy asked. "How can I make sure they'll never be hurt?" In true grandmotherly spirit, I shared the benefit of all wisdom collected since my own new parent dreams. In other words, I made a helpless gesture with my hands and replied, "You can't!"

Life is lumpy. "And a lump in the oatmeal, a lump in the throat and a lump in the breast are not the same. One should learn the difference."[1] Aside from basic rules of health and safety, teaching that philosophy is the best 'protection' any parent can offer. That, and praying each child can learn to cope accordingly.

Random tragedy exists. So does betrayal, injustice, malevolence and greed. Everyone faces hurt and disappointment; and no child—no matter how loved or how commendable its parents' intentions—can be guaranteed immunity from life and its pains.

Just as no one can be guaranteed safe passage in a world where madmen open fire in public buildings or bomb day-care centers to make a political statement.

Isn't hindsight liberating? How easy it is to look backward and acknowledge the frailty of noble purpose. It is also easy, once responsibility for the children's lives has passed from our hands to theirs, to look back and admit that parenting is an inexact science where everything is possible and nothing is certain. Hindsight frees us to concede the reality of our powerlessness. It also allows parents to reassure themselves and everyone else that *all you can do is do the best you can*… and keep your fingers crossed.

Which is probably why, when asked, "do you wish your kids were little again?" people with grown children often heave a sigh of relief and reply, "Hell, no!"

Not that most parents wouldn't do it all over again if given the choice. Their response, however, has nothing to do with repeat performances. Nor is it particularly related to loving—or even liking—one's children or being proud or disappointed how they turned out. "Hell, no!" is simply a healthy acknowledgment that: (1) children are supposed are to grow independent and away. And (2) startling to the kids as the idea may seem, parents have a right to get on with—and enjoy—the rest of their lives.

Yet knowing and feeling are two different things. Much as no-longer-actively-employed parents love talking about how they're enjoying themselves, people with grown children can be embarrassed about it, too. It is as if savoring their well earned freedom somehow makes them derelict in their duty… and they feel guilty that they feel so good.

Perhaps that is because, when it comes to family, stability is frequently confused with stagnation. The appropriate goal is to raise children to be independent; so appropriate interaction, financial or otherwise, is not the same between parents and their five-year-old as it is when the kid is ten, twenty or forty-five. Yet, if we acknowledge that truth, and rightly act upon it, from whence come the naysayers? Those who insist that parents—like Hallmark—should be 'the gift that keeps on giving.' That children, like Peter Pan, should remain children… and keep on taking. And that the natural order of things, a child's becoming self sufficient, defies abiding love and flies in the face of convention.

Perhaps the more appropriate question is *who conjures up these conventions in the first place?* Of course no one wants to see their grown child set up housekeeping in a cardboard box. And certainly parental interest in a child's welfare does not cease when the kid reaches majority. But where does personal responsibility on the parent's part end and personal responsibility on their offspring's part begin? Where does lending a hand to an adult child in crisis end and freeloading begin? And how did the lines get blurred?

Did the blurring originate from the same misguided ideology that says parenting youngsters is an always-delightful experience? And were both ideas the brainstorm of some kid with an itchy palm and an overblown ego? Whatever their origin, this is a perfect example of how untruths or half-truths repeated often enough can ripen into guilt-laden—but often accepted—cultural folklore. Unfortunately, when myths are mistaken for reality: the unwholesome can masquerade as healthy, bias can appear to be fairness, the impossible can be seen as doable... and everybody goes a little crazy.

From the late Erma Bombeck to Dr. T. Berry Brazelton, the notion that parenthood is unerringly wonderful has been repeatedly challenged. In addition to quality commentary such as theirs, however, are countless tomes that, whether technical or tongue-in-cheek, read like furtive missives from the underground. What is too often implied is that subject matter is akin to revealing a dirty little secret. And what is too often missing, is strong, illusion-shattering reassurance for parents under siege. Of course, bringing up children can give times of incomparable joy; it can also include some ice-cold doses of reality. Parents have a right to know their conflicting experiences and emotions are neither unusual nor immoral.

An infant welcomed with open arms can still be the cause of financial worries and/or drive its parents mad from sleep deprivation. A much loved toddler's tantrums can make family members want to run for the hills. The brightest youngster's academic problems can disrupt an entire household. And adolescents can cause unimaginable heartache by making decisions that range from unethical to dumb to downright dangerous.

It is not just worrying whether the kids have wrapped their car around a tree. According to the *Wall Street Journal,* when AT&T surveyed senior managers about their chief anxieties, "... teenagers were the No. 1 concern off the job and the No. 1 distraction on..."[2] Putting a human face on said distractions, the same article quotes a contemporary mother: "Do I go home and make sure my kid is really at practice and not hanging around getting stoned, or do I sit at work and hope for the best?" It also describes some of the perils which terrify today's parents, "... the accessibility of more addictive and hazardous drugs, for example, and the early age... that most kids now begin experimenting with alcohol."

Add AIDS to the list, and teen pregnancy and so on, and the issue of trusting one's children becomes moot. In its place is hard reality about the decisions every teenager confronts on a daily basis. All of which make it easy to understand the above-mentioned mother's belief, "You have to expect the worst. It's always nicer to be pleasantly surprised than paralyzed by shock."[3]

What is not easy to understand is the popular and guilt-ridden acceptance of another myth: the one which contends *parents hope child-raising years will never end.* That *had* to have originated from a childless source. Who but the uninitiated could be so naive? Just as who but non- or yet-to-be parents could believe *my kids would never do a thing like that.* Yet-to-be's determine with time, however, that there is nothing their kids wouldn't do. And never-enders discover that the world does not collapse because children grow up. Besides, they're going to do it anyway... but none of this means the myth is harmless.

The never-end concept confuses the savoring of childhood's precious moments with stifling an offspring's right to autonomy. It also sentimentalizes the latter as the mark of a loving parent. "I would never kick my son out of the house," a neighbor sniffed to a couple whose son had graduated college and was now leaving for a job on the coast. Meanwhile, sniffer's kid, a thirty-something, still lived at home rent-free and had trouble staying employed.

Another couple described their twenty-something's resistance to living his own. "You don't realize how expensive is for young people out there," he pleaded. And his mother retorted, "What do you think we get, a discount?" The parents held firm. The son was launched. Yet later, his dad nearly choked when he heard a colleague defend his own still-at-home-twenty-and-thirty-somethings with, "You don't realize how expensive is for young people out there."

Experts label such family dynamics—parents like the sniffer and the defender and their resulting adult sponges—as a 'failure to launch.' What a marvelous analogy... and what a sad commentary. Few would argue that being Mommy or Daddy to adoring, adorable little ones can be one of life's treasures. But no one has the option to freeze-frame time in order to keep the kids little. Condoning a growing or grown child's shortcomings, or fostering his/her dependency in the name of love, should not be an option either. Devotion to one's children is not the same as mollifying childish demands. And never should it be confused with satisfying a parent's need to control or need-to-be-needed.

Emotionally healthy parents understand that their children are neither possessions nor extensions of themselves. They readily accept that, while family members share a common history, each child's future is his/hers alone. They are also quite capable of dealing with life's inevitable passages and cycles. But most important of all, in spite of predicted loneliness, by the time the kids are out of their teens, the majority of parents are nearly out of their minds and more than ready to let go. A fact which should finally put to rest that patriarch of family myths, 'The Syndrome of the Empty Nest.'

Frankly, I thought that myth was long dead and buried... until I recently heard the psychological effects of profound personal loss described as *being like a forty-five-year-old woman whose kids have left for college.* Apparently, in spite of today's dynamic senior citizens, the sheer number of contemporary younger women in the workforce and the welcome involvement of fathers in children's lives, things haven't changed a whole lot since my own kids were babies.

Back in the deep, dark fifties and sixties, hardly a day went by without some magazine or newspaper forewarning young mothers to *enjoy your children while you can... because twenty or so years down the road, life will be meaningless and bleak.* The future envisioned for us, once our children had the nerve to grow up, was one where our days would consist of wandering aimlessly from room to empty room. No one ever mentioned we might be jumping in the air, exchanging high fives with friends and/or lovers or husbands... and shouting, "YES-S!"

In fact, husbands and/or the children's fathers were rarely mentioned at all. They were off doing important things like having jobs.

The antidote to an empty nest, we mothers were advised, was to not make our children the center of our world. At the same time, we were cautioned that pursuing additional interests was tantamount to neglect... and mothers who worked outside the home were self-centered, unfeeling, unfeminine aberrations.

Perhaps this myth and the related fall-out originated with some recruiter for unscrupulous psychiatrists. Its mixed messages sure drove people nuts. On the other hand, maybe Empty Nest was the brainchild of obstetrical brotherhoods. More than one of the women I knew decided to get pregnant each time her youngest child reached school-age... just to ward off the inevitable. In any event, whether it was leaving for kindergarten or college, a child's growing up or going his/her own way was seen as motherhood's darkest moment. *Finis!* The end! Better start twiddling those thumbs!

Strange, isn't it? After every national tragedy, from plane crashes to schoolyard shootings, media-types shamelessly rush the grieving process, touting memorial services as being held so families can 'get on with their lives.' Re: Empty Nest—does this mean then that parents are supposed to get over losing their children to catastrophes but not to college? To death but not to life?

The problem with myths is that they cater to the unwholesome. Yes, there are parents who refuse to let go... and adult-children who spend years on a therapist's couch learning to spit in their eye. There are also children who refuse to let go. *It's too expensive out there. Take care of me, Mommy / Daddy. You owe me. And while you're at it, take care of my kids.* There are professionals who shake their heads at such infantile paralysis; yet there are also those who should know better, but who perpetuate the myths because doing so is easy, convenient, sometimes lucrative and can relieve them of responsibility. The mother of a thirty-year-old hospitalized for depression was appalled when the man's physician (1) addressed her as "Mommy" and (2) demanded she tell him why her son hadn't followed such-and-such an order. She told the MD, (1) that she'd outgrown mommy status when Richard Nixon was still in the White House and (2) to ask his patient.

The Empty Nest myth plays a significant role in all of the above; yet, no matter how much credibility any fable has amassed, it remains just an untruth or half-truth with terrific public relations. Parents who are overwhelmingly needy, controlling, afraid of loneliness, or convinced that letting kids grow-up is synonymous with failure often encourage outrageous demands from their grown offspring. Or enable them. Or at least cannot resist them. They are also vulnerable to people like the aforementioned doctor. The result is, they damage themselves and do their adult children no favors. Crippling people with 'kindness' cripples them just the same.

But let's talk healthy. Yes, an after-child house can take getting used to. The silence can be deafening... until one remembers so was the music. Yes, an after-child house is different. But different is not a measure of bad or good, it is just different. Yes, a sudden sense of freedom can be disconcerting... until parents savor the good, throw off the discomfort—and perhaps their clothes—and realize the Empty Nest is but an empty fairy tale.

Once upon a time, we delighted in toddlers who lifted our sleepy eyelids to ask, "Are you in there?" Once upon a time, we loved it when our youngsters piled into bed with us on weekend mornings to roughhouse and watch a zillion cartoons. Now, in the happily-ever-after, it is sheer heaven to read the weekend papers and drink our coffee in bed... and only get up if and when we feel like it.

Once upon a time, my husband took his three- and four-year-old daughters to Disneyland. They were so cranky, he swore no return visits until they were teenagers. In the sequel, we took the older daughter and our son back to celebrate their high school graduation. They did not want to be caught dead in our company; yet they also complained of boredom when we agreed they could go off independently. In the happily-ever-after, husband and wife have taken a couple of Disney trips on our own. Against the backdrop of Mickey Mouse—and parents trying to grapple with whining, contrary youngsters—we had the kind of fun that kids are supposed to have, but only grown-ups know how.

Once upon a time, I cried the day my youngest child started kindergarten. *He's growing up too fast,* I argued with the wind, then dried my tears and watched my baby go as I had his brothers before him. After thirty-four years of mommyhood, however, and after raising three kids and two step-kids, the day the youngest graduated college I was neither crying nor humming *Pomp and Circumstance.* I was singing the *Hallelujah Chorus!* The season had come. It was time.

Hallelujah! Hallelujah! Hallelujah!

✍

1. Robert Fulghum

2. Working Parents' Torment: Teens After School. Ellen Graham. Wall Street Journal. May 9, 1995

3. Ibid.

Toss the Laundry List Into the Garbage

And the Blame Game to the Wind

What a wonderful invention is the Laundry List. No, not the sort which checks off panties, tee shirts and even two of each sock-pair before one gets eaten by the washing machine. The other type of Laundry List. The dual-purpose, emotional kind which censures but seeks no solutions, yet grants absolution to its creator.

The goal of an emotional Laundry List is to wash away personal responsibility. Focusing on the real or imagined imperfections of everyone else, it can be long or short, specific or all encompassing and can have its basis in truth, half-truths, misperception or deliberate fabrications. All Laundry Lists have one thing in common, however, every disillusion or disappointment which has challenged its author is another person's fault.

Those who care the most are often those whose names appear on the List. Who but a 'loved one' could be expected to give credence to—or a damn about—another person's catalog of reproach? And who else would be susceptible to a launderer's built-in guilt dispenser? It's the latest twist in a time-worn concept. Batterers have long claimed it's not their fault—their victims provoked the abuse. *I wouldn't have to drink if you didn't nag me about it* is basic alcoholspeak. Yet, much as dancing out from under is frowned upon and discouraged, shifting blame remains alive and well and just as miserable as ever.

In its currently popular version, twenty-, thirty- and even forty-somethings are encouraged to come to terms with life by looking back in anger. Then, by retrieving, perhaps reinventing and definitely nurturing childhood's grudges, they confront their astonished parents with the dirty laundry:

> "When I heard you say, 'both my girls are smart and talented,' I heard you saying I was insignificant as an individual and alone I didn't possess qualities worth noting. ...
>
> "When you say, 'I don't mind buying clothes for you as long as you're going to wear them,' I heard you say that spending money on me was a waste of money." [1]

Never mind if the long-ago message received in no way resembled the message which was sent. That is irrelevant. Parents are exhorted to just shut up and listen. The Laundry List is a healthy cleansing of the soul.

Whose health? Surely not those being held accountable for time-distorted history or being force-fed the stuff of ulcers and hypertension. And whose soul? Surely not those who view the world through inverted, infantile lenses or whose seething version of the past borders on paranoia. The young woman quoted above, for example, concluded her exposé with, "Today, I choose to recognize these things for what they really are: blatant child abuse... I use my anger about them as a source of strength."[2].

I Corinthians 9:11 counsels, "When I was a child, I spake as a child, I understood as a child, I thought as a child: but when I became a man, I put away childish things." Anyone who is old enough to vote, thus help decide the fate of a nation, and old enough to legally enjoy sex, credit cards and all the other so-called perks of adulthood, is old enough to put away childish things. Instead of alternating between rage and whining, or wallowing in condemnation, Laundry Listers would do better calling 9:11.

Apparently, they'd rather not. It is more fun operating from the premise that everyone (but especially me) is entitled to an easy ride. Never mind that life offers no guarantees or the luck of the draw is not always so hot. Those with a misguided sense of entitlement can: (1) blame the past because today's world does not cater to their personal demands, and (2) condemn whoever is 'responsible' for this alleged deprivation.

And who makes a more convenient scapegoat than those whose job it was to pave the way? If all of life's woes and setbacks can stem from mom or daddy having done or said the wrong thing, or too much or too little, one never need look in the mirror. Add self-pity to the list, and the difference between human frailty and parental crimes becomes indistinguishable... with both conveniently stuffed into a one-size-fits-all bag of dirty laundry labeled abuse.

Abuse has become the most abused word in the English language. And what a malicious, contorted play on words that is. In its newest interpretation, anything short of guaranteed, perpetual happiness fits the bill. Worse still, mere accusations of abuse are sufficient to condemn and even prosecute parents, guilt or innocence is immaterial and so is the magnitude of any alleged crime. Not only does this marginalize the experience of those who've truly suffered, it thwarts rational thought and erases civil lines of demarcation. Refusing to go bankrupt to meet a kid's expectations of popularity is not the same as rape. Neither is maiming or starving a child on a par with assigning reasonable chores. Yet under the credo of blanket accusation, all parents are created equal. Everyone is an abuser.

Parenthood does not confer instant sainthood on men and women. But neither does it make them automatic sinners. Mothers and fathers can be (and often are) bumblers and frequently make mistakes. They may even hurt their children's feelings from time to time. Yet accepting that one's mom and daddy aren't faultless is supposed to coincide with kindergarten. Or at the latest, puberty. Does it make sense for adults to seethe over their parent's imperfections decades after the fact?

Besides, filial relations are not a one-way street. Some parents suffer the misfortune of producing immoral children. Laying claim to child abuse in order to work out a personal vendetta or justify one's own shortcomings is the essence of immorality. So is fabricating such tragedy for emotional or financial blackmail.

Helping true victims come to terms with their past is

absolutely necessary; but even this objective has gone off track. Somewhere between getting angry, getting it in perspective and getting on with life, things have gotten stuck in getting even. Thus has evolved the Blame Game, a destructive, tyrannical horror show which presupposes that all parents delight in devouring their offspring.

The Blame Game equates to the world's longest temper tantrum. Fueled by compulsions to condemn, it is played with chips from its team-members' shoulders. The rules are simple:

(1) The only way to make the team is to have such a chip; therefore, if one doesn't belong there, it has to be invented.

(2) Facts and/or mitigating circumstances regarding parents cannot be considered.

(3) Compassion is disallowed. And

(4) Players are free to interpret their filial histories in the most excessive, ill-gotten, self-centered terms.

Perhaps a failing marriage shattered one or both parents and temporarily left them terrified. Perhaps Daddy lost his job or Mom was pregnant with her third child in five years and caring for her dying mother-in-law at the same time. Under a blamer's Victim's-Bill-of-Rights, there can be no understanding... even in retrospect. On the contrary, all childhood experiences which fail to mimic *Leave it to Beaver* can be retroactively categorized as abuse.

Given that set of standards, even the Cleavers would come up short. Upper-income parents were abusive for being a tough act to follow. On the other hand, children from average- or lower-income families suffered deprivation... even if it was of designer jeans or sneakers which cost more than the rent. Parents who tried shielding kids from trauma abused them by not telling the truth; but those who did not spare them were cruel for causing unnecessary anguish. Parents who blew their cool (even rarely) were abusive, especially if they said naughty words; yet those who never lost their tempers intimidated their children by appearing too controlled, too emotionless or too perfect. Those who participated in school and recreational activities were overbearing, domineering and interfered with the youngster's self esteem; conversely, those who found it impossible to be in two places at once were guilty of abandoning their child's inner needs. *Ad nauseam.* Evidently the only way a parent can avoid being targeted by the Blame Game is to have not had children in the first place.

It is a ruthless, no-win situation. Not only because of absurd, unyielding, ill-gotten regulations, but because the game is also played with an unassailable trump card: The word 'denial'... in concert with the phrase 'in denial.'

Denial is a valid word, as in protest of innocence. It is also an appropriate psychological term, as in a barrier against overwhelming pain. Denial is an integral stage of grief for example, and addicts who cannot admit they are hooked are described as 'in denial.' When applied to the Blame Game however, denial becomes a clever, sadistic, fool-proof method of crippling one's opponent.

Most people who are confronted with blatant lies or decades-old grudges are initially too stunned to answer. But if and when accused parents try to respond, anything short of an anguished confession is considered 'denial.' Never mind if the allegations are nonsensical or not true. Never mind if explaining certain circumstances could clear up a misunderstanding. Redefining denial to fit the Blame Game puts a new spin on abuse of power: accusers have full immunity and the accused are denied their right of self defense.

And so we conjure up Denial Abuse, a simultaneous bastardization and parody of Miranda Rights: *Anything you've ever said and/or done, and anything I charge you with or think you may have meant, and even things you did not do but I feel like saying you did... can and will be held against you.* But the tentacles of denial abuse do not stop there. A friend attended a grief support group shortly after her mother's death. Sharing the fact her present sense of loss was more intense than when her father had died, she also noted her Mom had been an encouraging, demonstrative parent while her Dad was temperamental and aloof.

Later, the facilitator handed her a copy of *The Courage to Heal.*[3]

Initially, my friend was unaware the book was a recovered memory 'bible' and that its main topic was incest. Once she started reading it however, she became furious. "Why did you give this to me?" She confronted the facilitator. "My father may have had many faults, but he did not abuse us. And he was definitely not a molester." A sympathetic embrace accompanied the condescending reply of, "You are in denial."

How have we arrived at this mass hysteria? This mandatory, universal membership in Adult-Victims-of-Whatever? This insistence that those who say their parents were not abusers are in denial? Survivors of child abuse used to be driven nuts by theories which discounted their experiences. *Your parents tried their best* was cold comfort to those who had faced the truly horrible. Today, however, in order to validate the abused, we invalidate any other type of relationship and demand mass confessions of the grotesque.

Are there no shades of gray? Is there no room for moderation or good sense? The status of children reflects each generation's social climate. American youngsters once fought in wars and worked twelve-plus hour days in factories at the same age today's children compete in Little League. But even though the idea of child labor and pre-teen soldiers is appalling by today's standards, last century's parents were not deliberately trying to do in their kids.

And neither were the parents who raised today's adults, even if they believed in philosophies no longer in vogue. Child rearing theories have crisscrossed the spectrum from "children should be seen and not heard" to total permissiveness. But *different* is not synonymous with *destructive,* and yesterday's decisions cannot be measured by today's standards. Outdated parenting practices no more equate with deliberate abuse than pop-culture is an acceptable bench-mark by which to measure it. As a society, we've been had.

One way we've been had is that abuse itself has become a powerful, profitable business with many subsidiaries. First, there is the mental health industry... and it is exactly that, an industry. It deals in commodities and competes within itself for market share. Unfortunately, its commodities are human psyches, market share is comprised of those who own them, and industry-wide solvency depends upon adapting an imprecise science to fit current notions, phobias and political agendas.

All of this may be reflected in the epidemic of sexual and psychological abuse stories which has assaulted our national consciousness since the early 1980s. While some of these tragedies are undoubtedly true, it is a safe bet many are not. That instead, they mirror a once-touted industry adaptation which is progressively becoming less credible.

Recovered Memory Therapy presumes with absolute certainty that each of its clients was a victim of abuse. No other milieu accepts assumptions as absolutes; yet, in order to even enter this therapy, candidates must have no recollection abuse ever took place. Instead, although memories gleaned in the highly charged atmosphere of therapy are not necessarily reliable, therapists 'lead' their patients to long-buried atrocities, and together they unearth them.

Such recollections are open to both suggestion and interpretation. They also presume that no hidden agendas exist and/or that all who seek therapy are people of good will. One need only match up a therapist who has unshakable, unrelenting RMT beliefs with someone seeking to validate his/her own specious behavior, and possibilities stagger the imagination.

And speaking of imagination, *The Courage to Heal,* for example, insists, "If you think you were abused and your life shows the symptoms, then you were. If you don't remember your abuse, you're not alone."[4] That is quite an indictment and quite an accomplishment. It manages to usurp the philosophy of Descartes' *I think, therefore I am* with carte blanche for every Blame Gamer who decides *I think it might have happened, therefore it did.*

Is the Blame Game the bastard child of recovered memory? Or vice-versa? Both reflect the malaise of social boredom. Both envision a world where all parents were villains. And not coincidentally, Recovered Memory Therapy also contains the stuff from which fame and fortune -- or at least big bucks—is made.

Since RMT burst into national consciousness, both qualified and self-proclaimed experts have peddled the idea through tabloid print and television. They and the alleged victims have basked in the guest-glitz of talk shows. Related confessional and professional books have sold off the charts. Advertisers have hawked Recovered Memory Therapy wherever there is space to be sold. Entrepreneurs have conducted seminars for healthy fees. Insurance companies have shelled out millions to mental health professionals. Public officials have used it to further their careers and private attorneys have found a lucrative new dimension to family law. Everyone, it seems, has benefited except those patients who have been ill-served by their therapists and family members whose lives have been torn asunder.

The mental health industry is not immune from unqualified, unethical or misinformed practitioners. RMT seems to have brought them out in force… the same way allegations of abuse seem to perpetuate witch hunts and hysteria. Symptoms of supposed childhood atrocities cover everything from avoiding mirrors (vampires result from abuse?) to neglecting one's teeth (guess not) to obesity to fantasizing to PMS. People who dare to disclaim these all-inclusive absolutes are told they are 'hiding from the truth.' Children, including adult children, who actually like their parents and siblings are dubbed as suffering from 'pathological devotion.' And parents who declare they loved and never tried to hurt their children are accused of being 'in denial.'

The list continues. Anyone concerned with presumption of innocence or Constitutional rights is 'protecting the perpetrator.' And anyone who has the audacity to question undocumented statistics, absolutist manifestoes or theories about human memory is labeled a misogynist or a child-hater… or worse.

In response, advocacy groups such as The False Memory Syndrome Foundation are now gaining both credibility and clout. It is about time. If the Berlin Wall could come down, perhaps this form of tyranny can be toppled as well. But it will not be easy. Recovered memory provides the delicious, seductive combination of pat answers, righteous indignation and big business. What better way to hook patients or sell lots of books than to affirm people's need to lay blame?

What a paradox. How are those who fall for the parent blaming scam going to react when their own kids jump on the Blame Game wagon and start accusing and condemning them?

Meanwhile, we have come full circle and ended up back at the laundry. For the parent who is confronted with the resultant List, the best bet is to read it with an open mind and give credence where credence is due. At the same time, require—no, demand—reciprocity: Insist upon a fair hearing. Do not allow yourself to be manipulated by guilt. Expect credit where credit is due. Then, tell your beloved whiners to grow up, or at least shut up... and toss the damn thing in the garbage.

✍

1. Making Monsters. R. Ofshe & E. Watters. (Charles Scribner's Sons, 1994 pp 22–24)

2. Ibid.

3. The Courage to Heal. E. Bass & L. Davis. (Harper & Row, 1988)

4. Ibid. p 22

Inherit the Windfall

or *How to Make a Monkey Out of Your Elders*

The commercial broke into the mellow mood of easy listening radio. *It's great to be fifty,* announced a female voice that sounded more like fourteen. *You're enjoying retirement, your kids are grown, and all your responsibilities are over.* Before I could shriek, "What?" or even wonder whose 'fifty' she was imagining, the voice continued, *so why not share this good fortune with your children? Spare them the stress of ever having to make painful decisions. Call 1-800 blah blah for your choice of 'Golden Eternity' burial plans.*

Ironically, I heard this announcement while driving to the gym for my daily work-out. But fifty-plus fitness is not the issue here, any more than is the wisdom of preparing for the inevitable... although both are concepts which I wholeheartedly endorse. What is pertinent is the distorted contemporary belief of 'you owe me.' Now even dead mothers and fathers are supposed to make things easy for their children. And be quick about it, too.

Sorry, children of all ages, there are some experiences from which even the most indulgent mommy or daddy cannot shield you. Somehow, the ad reminded me of the anecdotal rich man whose spoiled daughter was carried wherever she went. When asked, "Can't she walk?" He replied, "Thank God, she doesn't have to." Well, in this case, you have to. Stress is an inescapable part of the grief process. If your concern, however, is less about the pain of losing a loved one than it is about admonishing the eagerly-anticipated deceased not to cause extra problems, shame on you. Even parents have a right to consider more than the convenience of others when making final wishes.

They also do not unequivocally owe their grown children any part of what they—the parents—have ever earned, saved and/or invested. According to a syndicated article first published in the *New York Times,* however, current presumption is definitely otherwise.

Entitled "Clearing the Heir" when reprinted in *The San Jose Mercury News,*[1] entitled was indeed the article's operative word. Well researched, and peppered with so-called expert opinions, it glaringly reflected the latest gimme mentality. It was also guilty of what logicians call the Fallacy of False Premise. "Clearing the Heir" not only assumed aging mothers and fathers are parsimonious ogres who must be outwitted, it presumed grown children hold Divine Right of Ownership over their parents' worldly goods.

Viewed in context with the 'Golden Eternity' ad, this article had delicious irony. While burial brokers admonished fifty-somethings to be pleasant and make things easy on their kids, "Clearing…" bemoaned the plight of the very same mid-lifers trying to arm wrestle bequests from their aging parents. Talk about the sandwich generation!

My initial reaction was to try to convince myself the article was a joke. Failing that, I then offered silent thanks its author was not my heir... sole or otherwise. If she were, I'd sooner bequeath my entire estate to the Flat Earth Society.

Like the radio ad, "Clearing…" began with tender, loving belligerence. "Any way you cut it, baby boomers stand to inherit a huge amount of money." But don't spend Mom or Daddy's bequest in advance, the author warned, because "…with Americans living longer and remarrying more often, their estates are increasingly slipping beyond the grasp of their middle-age children."

The nerve of parents staying healthy and living their lives to the fullest. What right do they have to deny their grabby offspring like that? On the other hand, I shudder to think what alternatives these grown children have in mind. Apparently one set of sanctioned options is to lie, manipulate and make deals with the devil or his reasonable facsimile in order to get what one feels is coming to her/him. "What's next?" responded an angry letter to the editor. "Maybe some ideas on how you can get your folks to disinherit your siblings... or suggestions on how to use people you're not related to as well?"[2] That second point, though well taken, was actually redundant. The article did not limit the quest for a bequest to birth or adoptive parents. Through the miracle of possible inheritance, step-parents can finally achieve that long elusive recognition of their existence.

Recognition, mind you... not love or respect. One example cited a woman whose father felt he'd already provided generously for his children during his lifetime, and thus willed his whole estate to his wife. The daughter confessed to then maintaining some contact with her father's widow in the hope of becoming her heir. She even "invited her for holidays and once stayed with her for a few days to check on her health." Step-mom left the woman $79,000 in her will. The balance of her sizable estate went to acquaintances and distant relatives who, according to the outraged step-daughter, she "had to dig very deep to find."

Dig deep? How did the disgruntled daughter know this? And what made her more entitled than they? After all, what was her interest in the deceased besides wrangling out some death dollars? Did she really understand—or care—about the life of her father's wife? Perhaps these alleged casual acquaintances carried the older woman's groceries, or read to her when her eyesight was failing, or simply befriended her with no thought of reward. Perhaps they showed her genuine kindness or conjured up happy memories. Perhaps the older woman felt others could better benefit from—or better appreciate—her money. And maybe she was carrying out a grudge after all—although no one I know would pooh-pooh a $79,000 windfall.

In any event, it was the older woman's money to distribute as she pleased. With the exception of spouses and community property—or next of kin if someone dies without a will—no one is automatically entitled to anyone else's estate. Of course that does not stop people from believing otherwise. In a now-I've-seen-everything letter to Ann Landers, a reader told how her husband, who'd had been primary caregiver for his elderly parents during their final illnesses, was being sued by his siblings as a result. No, they were not claiming that he'd taken more than his share or that he'd cared for his parents in order to rip off the dying. On the contrary, their gripe was that he'd treated Mom and Dad too well. The elderly parents had wished to be cared for at home. They even wanted to enjoy an occasional 'luxury' like a gourmet meal during this time. And since their finances allowed it, the son saw to it those—and their other reasonable—wishes were fulfilled. Now his siblings—who'd never lifted a finger to help—charged that by allowing Mom and Dad to live out their lives in comfort, their brother had shrunken their parents' estate... and thus the size of their inheritance.

One more time, I shudder to think what alternatives these grown children had in mind. But back to "Clearing the Heir"... and to another noxious example. This time it was the story of a grown man who openly admitted he'd detested his adoptive mother. He also shamelessly confessed that he'd assumed the role of dutiful son for the sole purpose of inheriting her money. As a result, the man complained, he endured humiliation, degradation, indignity and threats. He also got lucky. The bulk of Mama's large estate was left to him and his daughter in a complicated trust... about which he remarked, "She wanted to control everything. The trust was a way to do it after she was gone."

Kvetch! Kvetch! Kvetch! His whine runneth over. Since there is no proof otherwise however, let us concede she really was the mother from hell. Does that make her conniving son any better? Neither the man nor the article acknowledged that befriending someone to extract money is both manipulative and every bit as controlling as they accused the deceased of being. On the contrary, a financial analyst/psychologist gave the guy "high marks" for keeping his mouth shut when Mama "sounded off"... thus getting the money.[3]

How comforting to know that so-called experts applaud the selling of one's integrity. And how uplifting to know the same analyst/psychologist advises approaching one's parents carefully when it comes to the subject of wills. With care, mind you, not with caring. "If you threaten a parent by saying 'You owe me,' and they are controlling parents," she cautions, "they will cut you off without a dime."[4] Excuse me? Who is attempting to control whom?

But one-sided power plays ran rampant throughout "Clearing the Heir." While sensitivity towards parents' feelings was encouraged, it came only within the context of not demanding the dough so the nasty old-folks would have no excuse to curtail your allowance—oops, inheritance. Nowhere did the article suggest maintaining a relationship because of the richness it could add to everyone's lives. Nowhere did the article allude to truly wishing one's parents or step-parents well. And nowhere did the author even hint that parents have a right to enjoy the fruits of their labors... and spend what they've earned while they are still alive.

Glaringly absent as well was any mention of how cruel it is for grown children to dehumanize their parents, hold onto childish grudges and/or to be "too busy" to write, call or give a damn. Instead, a Boston estate lawyer warned potential heirs to "keep those cards and letters coming."[5] because, so stated the article, "children who turn their backs on parents often end up with nothing." And a Los Angeles estate lawyer added, "One of the major reasons I've seen for disinheritance is the parents resent the children never visiting."[6]

Which leaves one to conclude that, in the realm of adult children and their parents, love, understanding and respect are out, and mercenary hypocrisy is in. So, apparently, are guilt trips, begging and ultimatums... since the article's resident psychologists and financial planners suggested heart-to-hearts about wills can "make parents more inclined to think about their children's financial—and emotional—needs."

How about suggesting those 'children' grow up instead? If a forty- or-fifty-something's parents have a history of caring and fairness, they do not need coaching from offspring... with or without an agenda. If, on the other hand, these parents have consistently shown real or imagined patterns of indifference and/or sibling favoritism, it is highly unlikely things are going to change much now... so accept it. In either case, it's a question of perceived parent-to-child obligation... and gee whiz, I thought mommy and daddy fulfilled their legal/emotional/financial prerequisites during the years of bedtime stories, braces and tuition.

The entitlement mentality combines overwhelming immaturity, complete lack of conscience and despicable ideas about owning someone else's money. Regretfully, entitlement's so-called experts reinforce that perspective by making it sound both logical and palatable. The end result is grabby offspring salivating without remorse over the bank accounts and possessions of parents they may not even care for. Frankly, I think these parents should (1) spend freely on themselves and enjoy life, (2) bequeath their money wherever they damn well please, and (3) sleep with one eye open.

Family ties can be complicated and painful. Sometimes a parent or grown child's alienation is not only for good reason, it is a key to survival. Sometimes the breach is unjust and unfair. Under no circumstances, however, can anyone be ordered to love, like or even respect another person. Even one's parent. And even one's child. Oh, such demands can be made, but that won't make the feelings happen. Besides, a relationship is a two-way street. So when it comes to parents—or whoever might bequeath you something—if you don't love 'em, or like 'em, or visit or keep in touch with 'em, they owe you nothing in return. And you have no right to expect—or demand—to be remembered in their wills.

There is also a case to be made for sincerity. Few moms and dads, no matter how strongly they desire their children's love, truly enjoy being kissed up to so that someone can become their inheritor. And many, no matter how much they want the family relationship, are quite capable of seeing around parental blinders. Any kisser then, who later found the ploy did not work, might try looking in the mirror for the cause of failure instead of blaming the deceased.

The difference between maintaining a relationship out of caring and manipulating one's parents or step-parents out of greed boils down to, *have you no shame?* To which many people can easily respond with an incredulous, *No!* And what if one was truly sincere and supposedly did everything 'right,' yet still ended up shortchanged in his/her viewpoint? Perhaps some re-evaluation is in order. The decision, after all, was the bequeathing person's prerogative.

Money is no more a measure of a parent's value than it is synonymous with love. Money may mean many things to many people, but no one is entitled to what belongs to someone else... in life as well as after death. A grown child's inheritance, whether substantial or modest, a surprise or something the heir has known about for years remains—above all—a gift. And gifts by their very nature have a right to be given freely.

✍

1. San Jose Mercury News, July 25, 1995. Reprint from New York Times/Jane Birnbaum

2. San Jose Mercury News, August 6. 1995. Letters to the Editor/Mark & Sara Perry

3. San Jose Mercury News, July 25, 1995—Quote Tessa Warschaw

4. Ibid.

5. Ibid.—Quote Alexander Bove

6. Ibid.—Quote Sandy Rae

On Life... and Loss... and Grief

In Memory of Our Beloved Gary

He touched so many lives. He brightened every room he entered. He was vibrant, brilliant, talented, witty, handsome, loving, giving, irrepressible and absolutely full of life. I want to remember him with joy... and most days I do.

I remember him as a beautiful infant trying to catch sunbeams that filtered across his crib. I remember him as a delightful four-year-old who dubbed regular- and king-size bottles of vitamins, "Gera-little" and "Geratol." I remember him at fourteen: a straight-A student who, when a friend gave him an air horn and warned him to *keep it cool,* took it home and put it in the refrigerator. I remember him at twenty-four, a gifted teacher passing his love of learning on to his students.

There is no social category for parents who lose a child. We are neither widowed nor orphaned, and language has no word for posterity turned into remembrance. So I remember: my son's first day of school and his college graduation. His love of sports and his disillusion with politics. His outrage at injustice and his outrageous, irreverent, non-stop sense of humor. He was a jokester, a mimic, a genuine impostor; and I remember him as 'The Man of A Thousand Voices" whose friends and family never knew, when the phone rang, if Bill Clinton, Big Bird or Dr. Ruth would be on the line.

Then there was an emergency room physician on the line...

and the joy our Gary imparted across the years as a cherished and devoted brother, a loving and beloved son, was shattered into a million, irretrievable pieces.

Lord Byron was right: "There is no joy the world can give like that it takes away." That call changed our lives forever. And, no, the happiness of having loved him does not always outweigh the sorrow of having lost him. He is gone. Nothing will ever be the same... and missing him is an immutable backdrop of the new reality.

Nevertheless, for all those who loved him, there is a new reality... for nothing is as awesome and resilient as the human mind and spirit. At first, grief meant unbearable pain. At the same time, an invisible, emotional shock absorber rendered everything unreal. Call it denial, being in trauma or anything else, but this is the built-in veil of human protection which mutes agony within hearts torn to pieces and allows numbed minds to do what must be done. Make arrangements. Write a eulogy. Brush your teeth. Then, as unbearable pain turned to bearable sorrow, grief's veil lifted slowly and step-by-step... whenever, as we all discovered, each one of us was ready.

Among those who mourn, this evolution can take weeks. Or months. Or the better part of a year. And oftentimes people do not realize they've even had the protective shield until after they no longer need it. Yet that does happen; sadness fades with the passage of time and, in the natural order of things, the mind inexorably turns toward readjustment, redefinition and healing. Even one's sense of purpose and optimism gradually returns... despite those somber assurances that 'you'll never get over it.'

Of course we will *never forget* him. Our futures will invariably hold reminders, happy and sad. So if 'it' refers to the loss itself... perhaps. But *never get over* the pain? Please, no! For that *never* is a devastating consignment to life without hope.

Equally devastating, cruel and emotionally unhealthy is the pop-culture notion that—from day one—the best way to deal with a loved one's death is 'get on with your life.' It can't be done. There is simply no way around the truth that time—and plenty of it—is the strongest antidote for bereavement and raw grief.

We do not do well with grief in our society. In fact, we never have. Once upon a time, by social decree, the grieving wore only black and were expected to lament for years on end. For the sake of the living, thank God those days are over. Yet also for the sake of the living, we might do well to acknowledge that buzz words like 'finding closure,' or expecting peak performance after three days of bereavement leave, can be as inhumane as expecting a widow to throw herself on the funeral pyre.

Grief is real. It is among the most profound of human emotions. We may want to downplay those things we don't understand or cannot face, but grief is a passionate, open wound that will not go away by setting time limits, prettying it up or pretending it doesn't exist. Death happens... and its outcome is non-negotiable. For the rest of my life, our son will be dead. Period. And that 'period'—that absolute finality—is the reason raw grief neither lends itself to platitudes nor responds well to pop psychology.

Nothing, not the best counseling nor survivor support groups, can alter the truth that there is no going back. Neither can they offer easy answers... nor should they try. For in a culture besotted with personal empowerment and hooked on trendy solutions, quick-fixes and meetings-anonymous, the starkness of death plainly shatters simplistic illusions. Grief forces us to confront the fragility of life as well as our own mortality. Further, and unequivocally, it forces us to recognize the reality of our powerlessness.

Perhaps that is the reason our society trivializes the pain of bereavement and tries to lump it into inappropriate, irrelevant categories. Yes, the types of loss people can undergo are nearly limitless and yes, there are many things to be sad and even grieve about and yes, there are parallel types of response. But it seems that current social thought is less attuned to cause-and-effect and more tuned to human response than it is to the human condition. All of life's pains and disappointments are not the same. There really is no common bond between the widowed mourning a spouse who died last week and someone whining about lack of parental affection thirty-plus years ago. Any more than there is a common bond between workers who lose a job and parents who lose a child... despite newspaper articles like one which ran shortly after we lost our son, where a young woman described her downsizing as, "It was like a death."

Perhaps the ex-employee's comparison, though overstated, was understandable. She was, after all, a twenty-something with limited life experience who was facing her first disillusion. But what about the so-called experts cited by the author... who callously and psychobabbably agreed that the denial, anger and eventual acceptance of losing one's job is the same as the devastation from burying a life partner or a beloved child?

Where are the lines of demarcation? Jobs are jobs. Things are things. If they cannot be duplicated or recovered, at least they stand a chance at being substituted or replaced. Those who've survived disasters with their lives and families intact are often the first to point out that no matter how much losing something hurts—and it can hurt plenty—and no matter how paralyzing or reality altering any event, as long as it is not life ending, life goes on. Just the mere opportunity to fear where one goes from here, or wonder if something can be prevented from happening again, holds the innate presumption even the most devastating upheaval can be temporary. That somehow other chances may lay ahead. The dead have no such options. And for those who mourn... well, I have been downsized from a job I really cared about and have buried my precious son. There is no comparison.

Yet among the bereaved, it is startlingly common to find the experience diminished or that they are isolated by their grief. Our family will always hold dear those who lovingly brought food, sent flowers, phoned, wrote sweet notes, stood by our side, hugged us and otherwise provided emotional aid and comfort. And yet there were those who, because they shy away from pain or truly did not know what to say, said and did nothing... and even avoided us.

We also shared the common grief experience of hearing thoughtless, absurd 'condolences' that leave one speechless. When a friend's seventh grader died of cancer, someone 'comforted' the little girl's mother with, "It's probably better this way. At least you won't ever have to worry about her getting pregnant or anything." Another friend, widowed with two toddlers at twenty-nine, was assured during her husband's wake, "Don't worry, you'll be married again before you know it." When someone else I know lost both parents within six months, her grown step-son cheered, "Oh boy, now you're gonna be rich." And a fellow church member called us to say, "I won't bother to offer support because I know you already have plenty."

Then there was the woman whose dog died a few months after our son. In all sincerity, she told my husband, "Now I understand how you feel."

With all due respect to pet lovers everywhere... many things can be said when a person dies. Most appropriate might be the simple, meaningful, "I'm sorry for your loss." There are also many things which should *never* be said, for this is one instance where the speaker has a moral obligation to think before opening mouth and inserting foot. People in mourning are especially vulnerable. Words that could otherwise be passed off as insensitive or just plain dumb can cause terrible and unnecessary pain.

It is also incumbent upon people to realize, no matter how badly they feel, that this is one situation which calls for all give and no take. For those at a loss for words... find some. Again, "I'm sorry" will do fine. At the same time, neither expect nor actively seek to be comforted in return. It may happen anyway. In fact, it is common—and possibly consoling—for the grieving to assume the role of grief counselor. But while it is awfully easy to let them, unless the needs of the bereaved are also identified, considered and being met, the situation can emotionally backfire.

During the tenth-anniversary Challenger remembrances, the widow of Commander Dick Scobie recalled how she'd spent the first two post-disaster years being strong for everyone else... then ended up being hospitalized for depression. Her story is not unusual. Blotting out personal needs, and acting as consoler rather than the consolee, often helps those in mourning to disguise and initially deflect their pain. But like every other problem in life, unless you eventually face grief head on it comes up and hits you from behind.

There is another sensitive area where thoughtfulness and discretion are paramount. Personal religious beliefs. The death of a loved one can cause even the most devout to question God's existence and/or feel cast aside and abandoned by their faith. In fact, doubts, misgivings and senses of emptiness and betrayal are normal—even usual—dimensions of grief. Well-wishers should also keep in mind that not everyone has a prayerful—or even God-centered—belief system to begin with. So no matter how sincere the thoughts, and while it's perfectly valid to offer prayers for all concerned, people should never, never impose their own religious views upon the bereaved.

When I went about the grim task of arranging to shut off of my son's telephone, for instance, the customer service rep signed off with, "You can be happy he's in Heaven now... and thank you for calling Pacific Bell." Part of me was startled. Part of me almost laughed. But part of me wanted to scream in pain, "How dare you say I should be happy? He doesn't belong in Heaven... he belongs at Candlestick Park!"

Not that we weren't comforted by the many prayers offered across all denominations. We were. But while wishing someone the solace of God's love is perfectly appropriate, insisting with absolute, pious certainty that those who grieve should be happy, or that the deceased is in a *better place,* or that a tragic, untimely death is *God's will,* is exactly the opposite. Never does anyone know that much, nor can anybody read the Almighty's mind. Besides, many earthlings consider this life the ultimate gift... and aren't so sure about the next. And many disagree that God's will includes untimely, incurable disease or that, to quote Dr. William Sloane Coffin, Jr., God goes "around this world with his finger on triggers, his fist around knives, his hands on steering wheels."[1]

In the same sermon, given after his son Alex's death in a car crash, Dr. Coffin also made clear how, "the reality of grief is the absence of God— 'My God, my God, why hast thou forsaken me?' " Yet he noted that even within such questioning and the depths of his pain, he knew "...that God is good." It is possible to mourn, doubt and have faith at the same time.

It is also possible to mourn and have a sense of humor at the same time. How many eulogies recall the lighter, funny side of a person's life? I know that the ability to remember our son the way he was, with his outrageous, irreverent, Robin Williams-like take on the world, helped to pull us through. And I know that our own ability to view life through absurd-colored glasses did so as well. Most of all, I recall that on the day of my son's funeral, those who we hold dearest gathered around my sister's dining room table and we all shared funny Gary stories through our tears. And I kept thinking, *Blessed are they who know laughter… for they shall sustain life.*

But humor is not the same as wanting to prettify things we don't understand or cannot face. Humor parodies life, but never does it say that bad things are really not so bad. On the other hand, downplaying someone's grief—and up-playing the divine—does. If there is an immediate, simple explanation for what went wrong (a là *God's will*) we can then assume there really is an answer. *God's will* also conveniently gives us someone to hold responsible, albeit lovingly, and spares uncomfortable bystanders from the pain of another's grief.

But there is no simple, one-size-fits-all formula for dealing with that pain… just as there is no way to measure one person's anguish against another's. Grief cannot be calibrated in terms of greater-than or lesser-than… for its dimensions are not measurable. Not only do a variety of cultural, religious and emotional elements influence someone's bereavement, there's also his/her relationship with the person who died. They may have had unresolved issues. There may be guilt. There may even be relief if the deceased had been suffering… and guilt for feeling relieved the ordeal is over. And clearly losing a relative one feels antipathy toward is not the same as the loss of someone beloved. Yet assuming it was a devoted, caring kinship—and aside from guilt and other feelings—how does one gauge the pain? Which grief is greater: from the loss of a spouse? A parent? A long-time lover? A sibling? A child? Is it more difficult to lose a husband or wife after a decade of marriage, or three or four? Is it worse to lose a mother or father who was young than parents whose death seems more natural because they were older? Is crib death any easier for parents to bear than a twelve-year-old's terminal illness or the sheriff reporting a grown son has been in an accident? Does it hurt less because someone's death comes from old age's inevitability? Or more to have a life cut short by illness, homicide, suicide, or a car crash? Do families whose loved ones' names are listed on schoolyard memorials or stitched on The Quilt or etched on The Wall hurt more or less than one another? Or more or less than we do?

Had Gary not died when he was twenty-eight and living on his own for several years, but when every corner of the house was still filled with his presence—and his stuff—would the pain be different? Probably yes, but does it matter? Likewise, does it matter if his brother's devastation might have been different had they still been kids sharing a room?

Perhaps grief can give us insight to the human condition. For while our losses spring from obvious, incontrovertible differences, what we have in common clearly unites us. Where we get into trouble is focusing on the disparities rather than the bonds.

Perhaps our most notable distinction was that at least we were spared one area of heartache. In piecing our lives back together, we could resume routine day-to-day existence without intensely appreciable change. But when loss of a loved one also means loss of a way of life, there is definitely a double whammy. Toys left untouched in a child's vacant room. The widow who must not only deal with emptiness and loneliness and perhaps single parenthood, but with social—and often economic—upheaval, too. And while a child's preceding parents in death defies the laws of nature and decimates the future, and while my husband and I have both read, heard and been told that this is the greatest sorrow one can experience, I've also asked my life partner and rock-and-salvation through our ordeal, "How would I survive if I lost you? Who would hold me when I cried in the middle of the night?"

I know I am 'lucky' to be able to ask that question. Nearly ninety percent of marriages do not survive the death of a child. It is understandable; for it is a time when each partner is hurting so terribly, and is so terribly in need… and neither has anything to give. It is also a time when flaws in the relationship tend to become unbreachable chasms. Perhaps by instinct, or perhaps because we just bumbled down the right road, my husband and I seemed to know this was a time we'd either have to cut one another some slack or we'd be cutting each other's throats. We chose the slack. And made, and kept, pacts that allowed us to express our pain and comfort one another, yet be honest when one of us needed a time-out or simply could not handle the situation. We never dreamed our outstanding ability to communicate was preparing us for something so profound. Or that it would someday be necessary to carry our partnership to another dimension. But it was... and we did.

I also never dreamed my career would help prepare us to cope with the loss of our son. Not that one is ever really prepared or that theory ever comes close to reality. But in both hospital and hospice public relations, I had written and produced brochures, newsletters and video documentaries concerning grief and loss. And that provided me (and consequently us) with the tools to understand what we had to do.

I knew the value of grief counseling and where to go to get the best. I also knew, to quote a hospice brochure I'd written, that "grief can make your world feel upside down..." and "... at times, you may be forgetful and feel as if you must be going crazy." In this case, my own words did not come back to haunt us but to help us normalize our topsy-turvy world. When something as strenuous as walking across a room left us exhausted, or if we were hit with sudden, unbearable sadness when a moment before we seemed just fine, or when anything, anywhere—like a news story about baseball's spring training—could bring on uncontrollable tears, at least we knew it was all part of the stages and dimensions of grief. It was the same when we couldn't even concentrate long enough to read newspaper headlines. We accepted that eventually it would pass, and it did.

From my personal standpoint, I 'graduated' slowly from reading headlines to short articles to individual chapters in a book to an entire book complete with a plot; and finally, to being able to read my own writing. That last step was vital because it allowed me to get back to work... although for a while my words and ideas read like they came from an infinite number of monkeys at an infinite number of typewriters.

Reading also became my antidote for grief-induced insomnia... except in the wee hours of one morning during my 'individual chapters' stage. Picking up Margaret Truman's book, *First Ladies,* I opened it to the chapter on Mary Lincoln, not remembering that she'd lost a child when in the White House. So I skipped to more modern times only to find that Mamie Eisenhower lost her firstborn to scarlet fever in 1921 and Barbara Bush's oldest daughter died of leukemia at age four. Then, I read about Jane (Mrs. Franklin) Pierce and Grace (Mrs. Calvin) Coolidge. Certainly my heart went out to all these first ladies in the way only another grieving mother can know; but by the time I read about the Coolidge's son dying at age sixteen of blood poisoning from a blister, I was actually laughing—at myself. I certainly picked a great way to take my mind off things.

Yet the book had a healing effect. It was one more example of how many people I know of, or know personally, who have lost a child... and survived. And that, at so terrible a time, one really has a choice. Mrs. Coolidge, for example, drew strength from faith and her love of life and "... within a few months of her son's death... continued to hug visitors, kiss babies, and shake thousands of hands, apparently with the same wonderful enthusiasm."[3] Her husband, on the other hand, was convinced that the boy had died as God's punishment for his father's presidential ambitions. Withdrawing permanently into grief, he declined to run for another term... and, within four years of leaving the White House, was dead at age sixty.

Unlike poor President Coolidge, we do not think our son's death was anyone's 'punishment.' Nor do we believe that God takes innocent lives for the 'sins' of others. And while it may not account for all suffering in this world, we simply accept that random tragedy happens. That inexplicable loss is exactly that, inexplicable. That sorrow is an equal opportunity employer. And that life offers no guarantees. In fact, among our very few certainties is the unprovable truth that Gary is always with us and an unshakable belief that he died loving us and knowing how much we loved him.

In *How Good Do We Have To Be*,[4] Rabbi Harold S. Kushner shared his own heartfelt insight on recovering from the death of a son. "There is a wholeness about the person who has learned that he or she is strong enough to go through a tragedy and survive, who can lose someone and still feel like a complete person. You have been through the worst and come through in tact." I found that passage to be particularly healing. And very, very special... because, from the moment we learned of Gary's tragedy, our family made a vow to 'choose life' and to come through in tact.

I also found solace—and a reflection of my family's covenant—in the words of the late Rose Kennedy. Years after the assassinations, an idiot reporter came across her enjoying a bike ride with a couple of teenage granddaughters. How could she actually have fun after so much tragedy, he wondered. And she told him, "Birds sing after a storm. Why shouldn't we?"

Indeed. Why shouldn't we? I know that the son whom we remember as irrepressible and full of life would want us to be keep him close through joyful memories, not grief. I also know that while we cannot forget his death, it is far more important to remember his life. Recently, his older brother told me, "I miss him so much, but I am coming to terms with him becoming part of our history." And I believe that says it all. His death was devastating, but his life was filled with beauty, and it serves no purpose but pain to think about what happened, or what he could have accomplished or what he might have been. So I will treasure what was and celebrate what he was, for my child of golden promise has become my Child of the Heart. His precious memory will stay with us forever... but the time comes to go on.

---

1 Sermons from Riverside— Riverside Church, New York, NY. January 23, 1983

2. Random House, 1995

3. Ibid - Page 253

4. Little, Brown & Co., 1996

II

Personal, Political and Miscellaneous Dilemmas

Over the Hill and Out of Your Mind

Growing Old Gracefully—Oh Yeah?

Age happens. Scientific advances cannot alter that fact. Neither can luck, good genes, healthy habits and/or and even an occasional face lift. Granted, combining any of those might create illusions of Shangri-la; but unless fate intervenes, aging itself is an inescapable, inevitable phenomenon.

That is however, age's only certainty. Otherwise, it depends upon who is doing the defining. Cosmetic advertisers infer that over-thirty is dangerously decrepit. Teenagers probably agree. On the other hand, at ninety-nine, our beloved Aunt Mabel calls my seventy-something in-laws, "you kids."

Then, there's my friend Phyllis. Two weeks shy of her sixty-first birthday, she was knocked off her motorcycle by a ditsy cab driver. One minute she was commuting to work through San Francisco rush-hour traffic; the next she was listening to a policeman radioing paramedics, "We've an elderly woman down on Market Street." Sprawled in the gutter with a broken pelvis, cracked vertebrae and assorted contusions, her cries were not from pain, but indignation. "What the hell do you mean, *elderly?*" she shrieked, and proceeded to lecture the startled patrolman, "Age is nothing but a number."

She was right... although 'numeric progression' may have been more accurate. Age does, after all, indicate an amassing of years. It is also conjugated in either the descriptive or future tense: old enough to drive... or to know better, for example. Youngster, mid-life or, as the Statesman Bernard Baruch replied when a reporter asked him how it felt to turn eighty-five, "To me, old age is always fifteen years older than I am."

There are times however, when the future seems to merge with the present. As all of us eventually discover, first, it's the sports heroes, then the police... then, even the doctors become younger than you. One's initial reactions may be surprise and the discomforting first inklings of feeling 'old.' With time however, each revelation seems to highlight life's contradictions and heighten our sense of the absurd. After all, what is more absurd than reporting to a boss who is younger than your first-born child?

That really happens. When I was in my late forties, the median age of employees where I worked was twenty-five and my department head was a week younger than my oldest son. At fifty, and with my career skyrocketing, I became eligible for the American Association of Retired Persons. Five years after that, with all our kids launched and my husband and I finally enjoying some 'disposable' income, I qualified for my first installment of senior discounts.

Note in passing: those twenty-something co-workers actually worried if it was OK to put "all those candles" on my 49th birthday cake. Assuming their concern was about my feelings rather than fire safety, I gave them the go-ahead. I also delighted in shocking them by wearing a San Francisco 49er T-shirt, cap and socks to the office on my birthday and announcing, "As long I've been drafted for the team, I'm damn well gonna wear the uniform."

The following year, I found plenty of "Fifty is Nifty" pins and stuff to mock reaching half-a-century. But five years later, there was no equivalent paraphernalia to mark becoming a senior citizen. Then again, there were those discounts... although it seemed a strange anomaly to be healthy, employed and even mistaken for my kid's older sister, yet authorized for discounts for no other reason than my year-of-birth. In response, I proclaimed myself a Junior Senior Citizen: i.e. *one who has reached that certain age but neither feels nor believes it.* I also joked that golden-oldie prices were a type of reverse discrimination and/or compensation for being 'over the hill.' Unfortunately, I was right on target.

Over the hill is a particularly virulent form of bigotry. It assumes life's peak has been reached, relegates everything past fifty into a warp-speed, downhill ride and lumps a multi-generation age span into a single category. Granted, the longer one is alive, the more likely it is her/his body will wear down... and out. But what about the months, years or even decades before this eventuality takes place? Offering a few perks here and there does not counteract the results of this lumping.

My criticism is not about Social Security, Medicare or any programs vital for senior survival. At the same time, I cannot help but wonder if those age-related price reductions extended by some stores, theaters and restaurants amount, in reality, to little more than throwing perceived old folks a bone. Getting into the movies for a couple of bucks less is not much consolation to a healthy, productive, yet conveniently downsized fifty-something who lost out on his/her pension. Nor do senior discounts mitigate the circumstances which allow such things to happen.

Of course it is nice to have such perks. And yes, I openly confess to taking advantage of them. But let's not kid ourselves. Extending ten—or even twenty-five—per cent off neither counterbalances the devastating effects of age-related bias nor justifies dismissing the accrued experience and individual value of a large segment of the population.

Ten minutes after author and columnist Joan Steinau Lester was asked to appear on a TV talk show, the producer canceled her out explaining they had a policy of no guests over thirty-five. "You couldn't keep the interest of the younger viewers," fifty-four-year-old Lester was informed. "Your book is perfect. You're the perfect person for the show... but we can't have you because of your age."[1]

Her experience is a variation of a very familiar theme. Whether this particular decision was the result of marketing lunacy or out-and-out discrimination, the author—like so many of her contemporaries—was astounded to find herself deemed antediluvian. She also raised a very interesting point with her question, "Are younger people never interested in the words of a fifty-four year old?"[2]

Never is a concept that one should never put into practice. After all, *never* includes you. A white bigot cannot become black. Anti-Semites can expect not to become involuntarily Jewish. Yet barring illness or accident, every person—regardless of arrogance—is going to get older. And though I do not wish to pull rank or sound condescending, I can honestly say, as long as one has the luck to be in reasonable health, *don't worry kids, it's not what you think.*

No one I know is going "gentle into that good night"... and not because they are raging "against the dying of the light"[3] but rather because that light is hotly blazing away. Ilona got her Ph.D. at sixty-five. Helen, seventy, teaches aerobics and jogs. Mid-fifties Harry and Gail moved half way across the country to begin new careers. And three years after her accident, Phyllis and her husband also pulled up stakes... not to retire, but to start new jobs in another state. My eighty-year-old brother-in-law Vic is still marketing his latest inventions. My friend Joan, after being operated on for uterine cancer, became a crusader for women's health. She also stepped up her time table for earning an advanced degree. Now, her picture in cap, gown and Master's hood—proudly surrounded by her husband, children and grandchildren—is on my bulletin board. It was taken the day after her sixty-fourth birthday.

Being a senior may indeed be a matter of years, which one cannot control. But it is equally a matter of attitude... which one can. Forget chronology. There are no limitations on staying young. Young has to do with one's sense of passion and compassion, curiosity, fun and resiliency. It does not mean having enjoyed an always-easy life. It does mean not allowing painful challenges—and even tragedies—to permanently dim one's brightness of vision or enthusiasm for living. It is all a matter of how one looks at things. On the other hand, it has absolutely nothing to do with how one looks.

Graying hair can be covered or not. That is a personal decision. Love handles can be dieted away... maybe. The market is flooded with alleged anti-wrinkle creams. But whatever one's choices about cosmetizing or hiding the signs of age, looks and looking-young still take a back seat to bias in the world of 'over the hill.'

Slender, shapely, late-fifties Kathy gets cast as sexy thirty-somethings in local theater productions. Off-stage, no one has ever requested ID when she's asked for her senior discount. In my case, since I had to offer proof of age to buy a drink until my late-thirties, twenty years down the road I thought they'd at least humor me or something. As it was, the first purchase I ever made with a senior discount was a weight lifting set. And the clerk (who couldn't know it was a gift for my son) didn't even bat an eye.

Apparently, there is a tacit agreement to ask no questions from those seeking senior perks. Yet one need only hear the patronizing, saccharine reply of "dearie" to realize the edict has nothing to do with respecting one's elders. Men and women who request a senior discount do not get carded—no matter how youthful they look or even if they are buying edible underwear—because no one can imagine people claiming to be *older* than they actually are.

Seniors do buy things like edible underwear, by the way. Many have healthy, thriving sex lives regardless of myths to the contrary. According to Helen Singer Kaplan, Director of the Human Sexuality Clinic at N.Y. Hospital, "Some of my elderly patients still enjoy good sex, although they can't always remember the name of their partners."[4] When the late Herb Caen had quoted Ms. Kaplan's findings in his San Francisco Chronicle column, he'd also retorted: "What's so odd about that? Sounds like most of us in our hey-hey days."

Caen, by the way, celebrated turning eighty by marrying his long time sweetheart and winning the Pulitzer Prize. Later on that year, disease, not age, ultimately took the octogenarian's life. "It took inoperable lung cancer, radiation and chemotherapy to finally make the man look his age." eulogized fellow columnist Stephanie Salter. Further recalling San Francisco's Herb Caen Day a few months earlier, Salter added: "At the end of the stage festivities... Herb situated himself behind the drum set of the Rick Martini Big Band... 'Oh, how nice,' I thought. 'Herb's going to play a little.' But Herb did not play a little. Bar after bar, chorus after chorus, the 80-year-old newspaper guy with lung cancer beat the holy hell out of those drums."[5]

Without doubt, Caen knew the secret of living in—and

embracing—the moment. However, getting back to the subject of what he dubbed "hey-hey days"... there is no way anyone can speak universally about over-fifty sexuality. Nor will I presume to try. In the name of writer's research, I suppose I could hang around senior centers and ask, "How's your sex life?" However, since I'd probably be propositioned or told, "It's none of your bloody business," I'll go with what I know:

(1) At ninety-two, Oliver Wendell Holmes, Jr. reportedly sighed "Oh, to be seventy again," as he eyed a pretty young woman. Notice he still noticed.

(2) We sent Phyllis a slinky, satin and lace teddy from Victoria's Secret when she was recovering from her accident. She and husband Jerry loved it.

(3) A couple married the same year I was born told an interviewer, "We still have it—the heaven stage—from time to time. It's quality instead of quantity, you understand."[6]

In the name of being cute about sex and aging, people often do a lot of harm. A *San Jose Mercury News* columnist, Murry Frymer, suggested we could learn a lot from his then sixteen-year-old cat, Hershey. The aging cat allegedly advised: "Three most important things in life are a) food b) sleep and c) sex. If you are neutered or a person over fifty, its, a) food b) sleep and c) regular bowel movements."[7]

Even if fifty-something Frymer meant that in jest, he should be ashamed of himself for promoting such a grim, dishonest stereotype. On the other hand, if the man really believes what he wrote, he should find a doctor or sex therapist, post-haste.

Myths about senior sexuality seem to come from two sources: Those still young enough to believe in over the hill, and those apparently so bitter, resentful and/or fearful about their own aging, they want everyone else to feel the same. The best sex at any age is based on mutual caring, desire and communication. If a relationship lacks these ingredients, or if a couple has spent a lifetime sniping at, abusing, or even ignoring one another, of course they are likely to have become turned off. On the other hand, people can meet, care and get turned on as long as they live. Forget Hershey. Loving and sexuality takes many forms and can adapt to altering needs along the way.

Each of life's stages has its own social and physical challenges. It is unreasonable to paint three or more decades with the same broad brush. A little child becomes a middle child, then an adolescent and an adult. And fifty-five can differ from eighty-five-plus in the same way newborn differs from thirty. Ask anyone who has ever held an infant in his/her arms. Or who has been caregiver for an aged parent.

Senior citizens are as varied a group as it is possible to be. Much is written about failing bodies, but many seniors enjoy robust health and/or remain physically active until very late in life. Studies focus on the ravages of geriatric illness, but sickness—and even death—is not the sole province of the elderly. Our culture also seems to equate productivity with one's era of re-productivity. But an awful lot of people with grown kids are still either fully employed or employable, and are in fact at the top of their form. Besides, some seniors are still busy raising children... and some are even raising their children's children.

There are also those who are having a ball in retirement and/or with their kids launched and swear this is the best time of life. Of course, such concepts defy conventional thinking. So does the idea of couples married many decades sharing loving and enduring contentment. That discovery actually startled University of California psychologists who'd embarked on long-time-marriage research believing in its disaffection and dissatisfaction.[8] What they proved was the folly of their own pre-conceived notions.

Mort and Shirley are one of those long-term couples. Laughingly, they recall she was aghast when he wanted to retire to Arizona's Sun City. "I don't want to be among all those old people," Shirley argued. "Not to worry," Mort assured her. "You'll grow into it." More than twenty sun-satisfied years later, both are so busy with all their activities it's hard to get them on the phone, and both reaffirm Mort's insight. Older is something one grows into... one day, one week, one generation at a time.

The biological clock does not stand still. And no amount of worrying, working out or deluding oneself that *everyone will grow older but me* will alter this reality. Our cells are not immortal and neither are we. Fortunately, the longer one is alive, the more likely he/she is to come to terms with all that.

Ponce De Leon, eat your heart out. Self acceptance is the key to a healthy attitude and acceptance of one's age—and aging—and even mortality *is* the secret of the Fountain of Youth. All of us are alive right here. Right now. Today. And life's greatest gift of all is the ability to find joy in the present.

---

1 San Francisco Examiner, May 21, 1995

2. Ibid

3 Do Not Go Gentle into That Good Night, Dylan Thomas

4. San Francisco Chronicle, March 28, 1995.

5 San Francisco Examiner, February 2, 1997

6 San Jose Mercury News, May 23, 1995

7 San Jose Mercury News, April 6, 1995

8. San Jose Mercury News, May 23, 1995

Oh, Yes You Do!

When Foot-in-Mouth Disease is No Accident

Social blunders are like the American Express Card—no one seems to leave home without them. On the happiest of occasions or in the most inappropriate of circumstances, people have a knack for saying the appalling or trampling on somebody else's feelings. Miss Manners offers an antidote: make offenders realize what they have said. Replying seriously—*I'm so sorry my being here reminds you of that failed financial venture*—to those who open mouth and insert foot, "...will then force them to retract it." Maybe so. But what if spiteful, gruesome comments come with malice aforethought? And how does one make the distinction?

Sooner or later, intent becomes apparent. Sooner or later, the difference between lapse in social grace and wanton assault sorts itself out. Leaving most of us with feelings best summed up by my friend, poet Mary Kelleher:

Why is it
That everytime someone says
Something nasty to me—
I mean Really Nasty,
I clam up
And can't think of a thing
To say back!

Meanies rely on rendering a target speechless. They choose

their word-weapons carefully... after all, without a retort there can be no retraction. What then is the remedy for people who find themselves tongue tied at the time and telling off the living room furniture for a week?

Perhaps yelling at the coffee table is the best they're gonna get. Miss Manners was asked to cite examples of ripping ripostes to one-up or shut-up the spiteful; but it is a mistake to think a facetious come-back will abash a meanie into silence. Truly cruel people engage in a battle of will, not wit. Unlike the social zero or someone who succumbs to nasty, impatient flashes during moments of stress, when genuine meanies are mean, they mean it. They want to inflict pain.

In order to respond to them in kind, one must get inside the head of the heartless... which can make the cure as bad as the disease. In the process of making amends to someone she'd wronged, a recovering alcoholic admitted, "I practiced the kind of manipulating, twisting and absolute cruelty that only the very sick can master." The behavior patterns of alcohol abusers and the willfully cruel are remarkably similar. The latter simply do it without the drink.

Intentionally mean people may be a breed apart, but they can be found just about everywhere: in the workplace, the shopping mall, the neighborhood and certainly among family members. Within their variations are true sadists... crazies who, as kids, tore wings off butterflies and, as adults, tear the hearts out of all those with whom they come in contact. Or at least get close to. Some sadistic behavior is compulsive; but most meanies understand precisely what they are doing and are very much in control.

Nasty people equate good will—or lack of bad will—with weakness, and their instincts are uncanny. They zero-in on vulnerable points and intuitively go for the jugular. Aware that treating one person with grace and another as garbage strips support and credibility from their object of disaffection, they automatically know who to brutalize and who to court. Nasties also understand how to play games with people's sanity and defy accountability in one fell swoop. If a target calls them on their conduct, stock excuses often begin with *I was just* or *I was only*—

as in *only kidding* or *following orders*—thus mitigating their own behavior and shifting emotional responsibility to the confronter. They keep a stockpile of retorts at the ready, too, including: *you're being hateful. You're too sensitive. You have no sense of humor. You don't know what you're talking about.* And *obviously something's wrong with you.* But rarely do they show genuine puzzlement at having been misunderstood or offer a simple, isolated *I'm sorry.* If one is unsure whether truly unkind remarks are deliberate, a perpetrator's intent may be detected in his/her reaction.

Then again, maybe not. Nasties are expert at making those who dare defy them end up with egg on their faces. They are contemptibly adroit at twisting truths beyond recognition. They can look someone straight in the eye and deny an incident ever took place. They are also masters at sulking, crying, affecting shock, becoming self righteous, getting angry or doing whatever else is necessary to extort an apology from their confronters. That way, they, the guilty-party-turned-innocent-victim, can be magnanimous... and forgive them.

Self legitimizing—making victims responsible for their own misfortune—is a basic meanie instinct. It is also a base one which reflects our society as a whole. Perhaps that is why cruel people feel they can act with impunity. I have a vague childhood memory of a comedian who, imitating a Dixiecrat Senator looking for causes of World War II, demanded to know what Pearl Harbor was *doing* in the Pacific in the first place. The audience loved it, but was his premise any less absurd than cold-bloodedly saying a mugging was the victim's responsibility because she carried a purse? Or inability to compete in the job market is the fault of fifty-somethings caught up in downsizing? Or one group's violence is proof of the other's provocation?

Sometimes subjugation trades the sharp barb for the sugar coat. Different method, same intent: diffuse, disarm, deter, detract, discredit and/or dehumanize. I once worked for an administrator who, when informed of anything from budget dilemmas to computer screw-ups, would stiffen, purse her lips and reply, "I can see by your body language you're upset." Next, she'd offer sympathy for the employee's alleged personal problems. If and when her psychobabble failed to divert the staff member's attention, the administrator would lash out and accuse the hapless informant of having caused the problem to begin with. Objections resulted in her further censure for being "too sensitive." About the time the employee was contemplating the definition of justifiable homicide, he/she would hear the saccharine voice repeat, "I can see by your body language, you're upset."

The tactic worked, if the administrator's objectives were to maintain absolute control and ignore anything she lacked the skills to deal with. Her problems did not disappear, but her employees did... with astounding regularity. And those who remained (as well as those who quit) clearly understood that, not only was Ms. Boss-Woman incompetent, her nasty streak stemmed from the fact she realized it.

The need to be controlling has its roots in feelings of powerlessness. The need to be cruel is the outgrowth. Although it appears to be an impenetrable suit of armor, the fragile framework in which the malicious exist is something over which they must exercise absolute control. Alternative thoughts, actions or ideas shake up that framework and threaten a meanie's security... and must be destroyed. What a miserable existence.

Meanies also live in dread of others discovering they, the meanies, are as stupid, inadequate or incapable as they perceive themselves to be. One school of thought is perhaps they shouldn't worry, much of the world already knows. But that is not necessarily true. Many people who hold themselves in low regard are not viewed that way by others. Their talents, intelligence and capabilities are apparently derided only by themselves. So it matters not if their pessimistic self-perceptions are correct. They are the defining factor of a nasty's being, a threatened, infantile being who sees the world only in negative terms of him/herself.

In the mind's eye of the insecure, everyone else's talents, hard-won accomplishments or simple good fortune exist only to make them, the meanies, feel bad. You lost weight to make her look fat! You sing wonderfully to prove he can't carry a tune! Your success shows she's a failure! Your competence shows he's a boob! Your kids are smart to make theirs look stupid! You thought up that bright idea for spite, since they didn't think of it first! No wonder they have to be cruel! How else can they defend themselves against your reprehensible ways?

The intentionally, habitually vicious are frightened, jealous, insecure and dozens of other uncomplimentary adjectives. So what? Their targets are not required to be sympathetic martyrs. Neither do they have to justify or excuse a meanie's secret agenda: revenge for real or imagined slights. Retribution for something which happened when both were children. Resentment because one married into the family. I hate (fill in the ethnic blank)s. Those on the receiving end could not care less about malevolence's cause. They just want to end its effect.

Forgiveness alone, unfortunately, cannot accomplish that... no matter how many times a meanie claims he/she's sorry. First of all, forgiveness is a two-way street. The now sober alcoholic who'd mastered the art of cruelty further noted that continuing recovery meant she'd had to "...come face to face with the past wreckages of my life and genuinely apologize to all those I'd hurt." The key word is *genuine*. People who willfully inflict pain on others have no room for anything like it in their vocabularies. They also find the ideas of admission or atonement debasing, if not incomprehensible, and mistake the word repentance for regroup. When committed meanies sense they have gone too far or a target is on to their tactics, they are not above apologizing to gain someone's trust; then—like Lucy, Charlie Brown and the football—whapping 'em again.

Forgiveness cannot alter the past. Nor is it supposed to... which makes bygone footballs irrelevant. Forgiveness is, however, about ensuring a better future... which makes it imperative that those who seek it really mean it. Otherwise, if their objective is to be absolved from responsibility, not mend fences, then faith in their good will can be ill placed. Or just plain dumb. The dumb point is masterfully made in the story about the boy who nursed a battered snake back to health, then cried, "How could you do this to me?" when the creature ultimately turned around and bit him. *"I'm a snake,"* shrugged the reptile. *"What did you expect?"* It is a good idea to keep that tale in mind when dealing with a perpetual meanie. And tread carefully.

There is no set formula for dealing with malicious people. The mastered art of a meanie is placing others in a no-win situation. A friend who lost a lot of weight told me about a guy who cornered her at a party and sneered, "We're all watching you and counting the days till you put it back on." At first, the successful dieter considered it her finest hour when she looked him in the eye and replied, "Thank you for your good wishes." Later, she wondered if punching him in the mouth would not have been better. Or if she shouldn't have disrupted the gathering by shouting, "How dare you? You S.O.B…" and/or told everyone the reason she was leaving, then walked out. But had she done what she later thought of, she would have upset innocent bystanders and looked like an idiot… and that is exactly what the perpetrator counted on.

The story makes a no-win point; but the episode itself was inconsequential. One can walk away from an obnoxious acquaintance. When the meanie has an emotional and/or financial hold on his or her victim however, the situation is far more complicated… and can have far reaching consequences.

People with abusive relatives, blood or in-law, often face censure from the rest of the clan if they say "Enough!" Singing Johnny Paycheck's, "Take This Job and Shove It" may delight the imagination, but is hardly practical no matter how trapped one feels in a horrendous work situation. And statistics on domestic violence are a chilling reminder of what happens when one is married to a meanie.

There is no easy decision in these types of circumstances. Every alternative appears horrendous and often is. When the problem is work related, practical advice such as *request a transfer, get another job,* or *document—you may have legal action*—can be well-meaning but just too simplistic. Overlooking what can be the magnitude of the dilemma, the advice assumes transfer requests are received without retaliation, downplays the common plight of 'whistle blowers' and omits the pitfalls of looking for work when one is wiped out from on-the-job battery. Being demoralized hardly sets the stage for knocking 'em dead—or even making a decent impression—on an interview. Such suggestions also disregard both legal realities and the statistics of seeking employment in a volatile, downsized job market. In one of life's stranger twists of fate, the victim may also need a recommendation from his/her tormentor. Meanwhile, people in this position face the daily choice between emotional, physical or sexual harassment or being unable to feed their families.

A similar dilemma confronts those with meanie relatives, including a sadistic spouse. Gut wrenching as it may be, acknowledging families have more to do with belonging than biology—and one does not belong where he/she is abused—ends up the easy part. Actually terminating relationships which encompass love, children, personal identity, long-term memories, strong filial bonds and/or sacred vows can be devastating... even when that is the only viable choice. It is also one thing to refuse contact with an abusive in-law or sibling, quite another to end a marriage. Beyond the shattered hopes and loss of a way of life, are such realities as scoffed at child support laws, fear of losing custody to an abusive other-parent, or women forced to provide for themselves and/or families on sixty-five cents on the dollar. Yet remaining in a dangerous, abhorrent family situation can literally get one killed.

People in emotionally abusive relationships have three choices: (1) knuckle under and be destroyed, (2) build an emotional wall so tough nothing can penetrate it, or (3) get out. The old stand-by, 'they are not going to change, the only choice is to change your response' applies here. Unfortunately, in star-crossed marriages, when a spouse tires of the first alternative and masters the second, the emotional violence often turns physical... so getting out is still the only reasonable, long-term choice.

On the other hand, while that choice is reasonable, sensible and sane, it is not necessarily safe. 'Getting out' is also precursor to most parental kidnappings and 'domestic' murders. Impatient, condescending theories about spouses who stay in abusive relationships cannot dispute that fact. Any more than belief in the legal system ensures that a man who kills his wife will be denied custody of their children. As a society, it is crucial that we take a long, hard look at what passes for family values. And that our laws develop some integrity as well as some teeth.

But back to meanies in general. From spouses and other assorted relatives, to obnoxious acquaintances, to the friend who really isn't, to a conniving co-worker, treachery is akin to rhythm: people either have it or they don't. A meanie will always be better at dispensing hurt and humiliation; and attempting to outwit one will always be exhausting, dehumanizing and an absolute waste of time. So will focusing on their injustices, ruminating about their persecutions or trying to make them accountable. Accepting those facts is neither cowardice nor caving in to cruelty. It is coming to terms with reality and the hopelessness of dealing with the truly cruel.

The malice is in the meanie. The only way to effectively silence one is to get him or her out of your life.

✍

Hear That Lonesome Whistle Blow

Secrets of the American Workplace

Voltaire said, "Work spares us from three evils, boredom, vice and need." That may have been true in his time, but most of today's employees swear their workplaces produce an ample supply of all three. How else could a dippy-looking nerd like Dilbert have become the icon of cubicle America?

Why this particular guru? Dilbert offers no management philosophy. He's not a feisty champion of worker's rights. His take on the state-of-the-art workplace is really nothing new... yet that is precisely why this cartoon character has become a prophet in his own time.

Dilbert is *Everyworker*. His predicament, as well as his bewildered, acerbic asides, validates the sanity of all who've ever labored in an arrogant, inept environment. Dilbert also gives voice to what employees have long felt in their bones: *The Peter Principle* is a standard, cross-industry policy and procedure. No one who has done hard time under idiotic management doubts that "in a hierarchy, every employee tends to rise to his level of incompetence."

Business wasn't exactly down, but Company X wanted to increase its direct marketing sales figures... so they fired the Director of Marketing. Never mind that he was an innovative leader who encouraged employee creativity and was highly respected by his staff. From upper management's viewpoint, he had this bad habit of honestly defining what was possible to achieve.

Within his department was a shortsighted, inexperienced underling whose main credentials were pie-in-the-sky planning and the art of corporate leapfrog. She suggested that the company increase its direct marketing campaigns from five to eighteen separate mailers per week. "That way," her proposal concluded, "we can boost sales figures even if our rates of response remain the same." The Director of Marketing pointed out that conceptualizing, designing, writing and producing these additional pieces would amount to a three-hundred-and-fifty percent increase in the current workload. In a snit, Ms. Ambition decided to go over his head… and after his job.

She reported to the O's (CE and CF) that her fossilized, employee-mollycoddling boss absolutely refused to implement her cost-free plan for augmenting sales figures. The Director of Marketing was called on the front office carpet. However seductive the scheme might look on paper, he cautioned, without a substantial increase in personnel, it was phony, unworkable and tantamount to stafficide. But the bigwigs did not want excuses. They wanted results. A single memo announced his termination and her promotion.

Ms. Ambition revealed the new marketing plan during her first meeting as department head. In quick succession, she then: extolled the virtues of her fifteen-hour workdays; demanded all underlings consider her a role model; reminded everyone of their 'exempt' status, which meant no pay for overtime; and smugly announced that there would be no additions to the ranks.

Staff was stunned. They attempted reasoning with Ms. Ambition. She accused them of being brainwashed by their previous boss. They used material data to verify the workload was impossible. She made it clear no dissent would be brooked and that anyone who did not go along was free to quit. Some did. Others, after weeks of feeling sickened and betrayed, figured they had nothing to lose and approached upper management… who responded by calling in an industrial psychologist.

The psychologist never questioned a single employee. Instead, he held lectures on the joys of being a team player and the evils of resisting change. Morale continued to plummet. Management switched tactics. Anyone showing signs of stress overload was warned what happens to troublemakers or found his/her services "no longer required." That Ms. Ambition and her plan might be misguided—or just damn wrong—was never even considered. Neither was the concept that people who do the work actually might know what they are talking about. When the scheme inevitably—predictably—flopped, the decision makers disavowed their own lack of judgment. Instead, they lay blame on an "uncooperative, unstable" marketing staff, took decisive action and promptly fired those who remained.

This may be the most absurd nightmare I witnessed during my career, but variations on the theme repeat themselves in workplaces everywhere and every day. Ms. Ambition promoted the idea of a fifteen-hour work day and management promoted her. In turn, she played both martyr and martinet by exhorting *I forego all other life... why can't everyone else be so devoted?* In Orwellian fashion, the company-paid psychologist then declared that sickness was health.

But sickness is not health, workaholism is not wellness, and preposterous projects will always be doomed to failure. Even when Wall Street cheers and corporate stocks rise in response to a company's downsizing, the impossible still cannot be made possible and forced exhaustion and threats of termination remain the antithesis of productivity.

In today's corporate culture however, employees are more likely to endure the tortures of the damned than to voice their protests. And those who might once have attempted to protect themselves or their staffs from institutional stupidity have gone from enlightened rarity to endangered species.

Perhaps they always were endangered. Studies have long concluded that morale and productivity can be enhanced by: (1) treating employees with respect instead of disdain, and (2) putting the overall good of the company ahead of anybody's ego. Industrial sages have also long cautioned that truly solving a problem works better than seeking a myopic quick fix. In turn, management has long given lip service to these concepts, then summarily ignored them.

Also ignored have been countless studies which identify workaholism as an insidious disease. Soul-robbing as any addiction to drugs or alcohol, it skews perceptions, alters reality, and damns both its victims and those within their reach. Yet the honor of work itself is indisputable... so the work-obsessed have the unique ability to hold themselves above reproach and disparage their non-addicted colleagues as moral failures.

It is one thing to have aspirations, love one's profession and/or bask in a sense of accomplishment. Quite another to be driven by blind ambition or a manic need to prove self-worth. Unfortunately, modern culture discourages the wisdom to know the difference. With all the lip service given to employee health and preventive medicine, workaholism is a public health menace which corporations abet, exploit and reward.

Likewise, with all the attention focused on family values, business has actually replaced the family as society's primary institution. Ask any employee who has been dressed down for having a sick child or a scheduling conflict between job and home. Better yet, ask my former next door neighbor. On the day she returned to work after her son's sudden death, her manager and an H.R. rep summoned her to a private meeting. "How long do you expect to grieve," they demanded. "After all, there is work to be done." This occurred, by the way, at a well known, highly respected Silicon Valley firm which brags about its 'family friendly' policies.

Bluster aside, contemporary business climates are not family friendly. Nor are they particularly reasonable in their expectations. According to author and career columnist, Carol Kleiman, "...in order for workers to survive in today's world, they should be accommodating, extremely flexible, fluent in many languages—it's a global economy—and master a variety of skills."[1] "It works for you because you learn more skills, but it works even better for the employer because it can get rid of five people and you can do six jobs."[2] Any bets on the sextuplet's job status if he/she ever recovers from certain nervous exhaustion?

Kleiman calls this six-to-one ratio, "dejobbing." Other pundits and observers dub it 'corporate anorexia.' Certainly the skin and bones concept is just as unhealthy as its non-workplace namesake. Also dying of starvation is the traditional working relationship where performance is rewarded with job security and employer loyalty... which accounts for the astronomical increase in the use of contractors. That and the combination of tax benefits for the employer and no benefits for the employee. According to Kleiman, employers no longer want employees. They've simply "... become part of the commodities that a business has. You buy them when you need them and you let them go when you don't."

There is something very wrong with this picture. Not with Kleiman's appraisal, but with what she is assessing in the first place. One can rationalize the necessity of demanding workers be flexible as Gumby and take on the impossible with a smile. But how can one ever justify the dejobbing based conversion of human beings into commodities?

Apparently no one dares to ask the question... or seems to care. No one seems to object that corporate cultures use the dysfunctional family as their role model either. But how many companies operate through control freak mentality, by distancing management from underlings and by pretending everything is well when it's not? And how many treat their 'old folks' as an inconvenience and/or impediment, and routinely put them out to pasture.

Laws against age discrimination notwithstanding, there is strong evidence that older workers are the primary target of corporate mergers and downsizing. There is also strong evidence that folks over fifty who are phased out of their jobs face the likelihood there is no place to go. Apparently being versatile in today's workplace is not good enough. Employees also need to have discovered the fountain of youth.

Getting rid of 'expensive commodities' may look good on paper. In reality, it is short sighted and bad for business. Older workers take their accumulated experience and knowledge of what has previously succeeded or failed with them. You get what you pay for.

One of author Scott Peck's descriptions of evil people is, "... they commit crimes against life and liveliness."[3] If throwing older, long term employees on the scrap heap and/or relegating all workers to the same status as pork bellies do not fit this category, they surely are a reasonable facsimile... somewhat akin to describing civilians killed in a bombing raid as 'collateral damage.' Both concepts commit crimes against life and liveliness. Both concepts devalue human life. Both concepts disguise cruel reality in a veil of words.

Disguising reality in the workplace is nothing new. Fundamental on-the-job principles have long turned humanity's guidelines inside out. In the Bible, John 8:32 tells us "The truth shall make you free." Yet telling the truth made the Director of Marketing free from his livelihood. The Ten Commandments include, "Thou shalt not covet" and "Thou shalt not bear false witness." But doing both paid off for Ms. Ambition and has for many like her. The workplace is definitely not a Sunday School.

Nor does it lend itself to other lessons. Philosophers suggest lighting one candle beats cursing the darkness. Yet front-office inhabitants are famous for operating in the dark because they allow themselves to see only what they want to see; and those who attempt to light the mythical candle are often cursed at or themselves end up cursing in frustration.

In an ideal world, preventing mistakes, saving money, revealing corruption or even true danger would be considered an heroic act. But in the virtual world, reality is not always compatible with management egos... and telling the truth can mean paying the consequences.

Books, feature films and TV movies romanticize the plight of an employee who stumbles into such a predicament. Faced with to-tell-or-not-to-tell, the ordinary Joe-or-Jane becomes the lead character in a morality play. *Silkwood,* which was based on fact, and *The China Syndrome,* which was fiction (but which could have been true), depict a worker's fate *in extremis.* In reality, someone is just as likely to uncover the Stupid Syndrome as the China Syndrome, but the dilemma is exactly the same.

Employees who 'blow the whistle' open themselves up to the possibility of humiliation, intimidation, strong-armed persuasion to 'forget it,' demotions, unwelcome transfers and eventual termination. In addition, since anyone perceived as a co-conspirator is subject to similar treatment, colleagues can turn cold in a hurry. Talk about finding who one's friends are... whistle blowers do not win popularity contests. Not in the front office. Not with middle management. Not with the person in the adjoining cubicle.

And talk about getting caught with your vulnerability hanging out. If 'doing the right thing' can result in an employee being fired, how many could—or would—actually choose ethics above a paycheck? Knowing 'the law is on your side' is of little consolation to anyone caught up in the to-tell-or-not-to-tell dilemma. Families cannot eat their bread-winner's good conscience.

Nor can they eat retroactively. True, many states boast Whistle Blower Protection laws. But employees know the court system is layered in bureaucracy, slower than molasses and outrageously expensive. No matter how valid or potentially lucrative anyone's case, the issue becomes how do whistle blowers *et al* endure in the meantime? Truth is the first casualty in the need for survival.

Integrity is the second. The deck has long been stacked against workplace ethics; however, the current economic climate makes it easier than ever for employers to skirt the law. A whistle blower can simply be marked for the next round of downsizing. This also reduces the probability that menacing—perhaps life-threatening—issues will ever be exposed. Employees who might once have considered speaking up are now more apt to adopt the policy of the three monkeys, even if what they are ignoring is truly evil. Labor attorneys also caution workers to never depend upon colleagues coming forward to support their claims... even under oath. It is not a question of the co-worker's loyalty to the employer. Nor his/her aversion to tattling. It is about money. When conscience is in direct opposition to survival, survival wins. And everyone loses. People instinctively protect what they perceive to be their own interests.

But whose interests are really being protected? Employees who ignore a fiscal fiasco could find their own jobs affected down the line... perhaps the company will go bankrupt. Those who disavow dangerous truths may end up jeopardizing their own—and/or their loved one's—safety. Besides, going along and/or keeping one's mouth shut offers no guarantee of immunity. In a corporate culture which turns its back on staff abuse, or commands workers to hush things up, an employee's only safe bet is that his/her time may well come.

One human resources manager oversaw a round of downsizing for a large organization. Although aware that certain 'budget cuts' were illegal, 'gotcha' vendettas, he kept quiet to keep his job. When the last pink slip was distributed however, and the final exit interview concluded, he was summoned by the CEO and handed walking papers of his own. As HR manager, he'd chosen fear and expediency over integrity... and lost anyway. Then there was Ms. Ambition. Thirty pounds heavier and with nails bitten to the quick, on the day she was downsized she whined to a co-worker, "This place grinds you up, chews you and spits you out!"

On the other hand, someone I know who—for years—has forlornly described her workplace as "the dysfunction continues," is still hangin' in there.

So the questions become: Does languishing in an outrageous work environment make one a participant in that environment or a victim of circumstance? Does ignoring mistreatment of a colleague endorse the injustice or simply protect one's self interest? Does averting one's eyes from imminent danger make an employee an innocent bystander or an integral part of the danger?

No one can extol the joys of integrity to those who may have to pay its price, any more than someone can legislate another person's morality. Sometimes every alternative is frightening and terrible, so it is unfair to pass judgment on anyone who must make such decisions. At the same time, every human act is the result of individual choice... even the decision not to act at all.

Hanging Dilbert cartoons on the bulletin board may alleviate workplace tensions, but it does not alleviate its problems. On the other hand, by his Everyworker status, nerdy Dilbert may indeed hold a key. Since his plight points out how all employees are governed by similar nonsense and frustrations, perhaps he'll awaken the sleeping giant of solidarity and cause colleagues to band together and back one another up.

Sometimes it even works. When the *San Francisco Chronicle*

and *Examiner's* management threatened to fire striking production workers, the newspapers' columnists declared 'they go and we go, too!' Likewise, in spite of overtime pay and masses of available 'downsized' to take their place, General Motors' employees successfully struck against unconscionable hours and workloads. Even in the lean-mean nineties, enough was enough. While not a blanket endorsement of all union issues, both instances are good leads to follow—there are ample supplies of 'enough' to go around.

Human beings are not commodities to be acquired and dumped at will. Harassment, intimidation, dangerous incompetence, coercion, and the seduction of workaholism are also unacceptable workplace policies. Young workers are going to get older, so age discrimination is everyone's responsibility... as is racial, ethnic and sexual discrimination, and an unresponsive court system which makes a mockery out of employee justice.

At the risk of sounding naive—and even preachy—commitment to everyone's interest is still an employee's best bet. Granted, it is often not the easiest road, but the alternative is no guarantee against unemployment either. And since one has to look in the mirror and the bell probably 'tolls for thee' anyway, it might just as well ring for integrity.

✍

1. The Career Coach: Carol Kleiman's Inside Tips to Getting and Keeping the Job You Want (Dearborn Financial Publishing, 1994)

2. Interview with Carol Kleiman. San Jose Mercury News. October 21, 1994

3. People of the Lie (Simon & Schuster, 1983) Page 69

Friendship is a Trip to the Wishing Well

You Can't Have One Without the Other

When her sister, Nancy, observed that sisters are one's shield against life's cruel circumstances, the late author Jessica Mitford is said to have replied, "Sisters are life's cruel circumstances." Naturally, neither is always so. Some siblings become lifetime confidantes. Others become crosses to bear. Still others form every imaginable combination in between.

Just as it is with siblings, so is it with friends; with the momentous exception that friendships come about by choice. The greatest compliment one can give a sister is to call her a friend. The greatest tribute one can pay a friend is to dub her a sister. Yet if non-genetic roots should atrophy for any reason, a friendship can run its natural course... if not always without regret, at least sans guilt, entanglements and the wrath of assorted relatives.

Hence we have one of life's supreme ironies: since they flourish in season and can fade if and when they are supposed to, kinships bonded by choice not biology bear the closest resemblance to Mother Nature.

As with all life choices, some friendships turn out not so hot while others prove durable and brilliant. The same friend who sat glued to the television with me through President Kennedy's funeral sat glued to my side when I wrote my son's obituary thirty-two years later. And we laughed a lot in the interim. My writing partner from two decades ago is still the friend I trust with my soul searching and for honest, objective critiques on my latest manuscript. We, too, have shared both pain-and-sorrow and joy-and-laughter over the years. In fact, one upside of being the same age as Madeline Albright is having such friendships that span large chunks of history.

Another is discovering, again and again, the truth of words learned long ago around a Girl Scout campfire, "Make new friends and keep the old. One is silver. The other gold." On the day of her son's marriage, a friend of a couple of years—not decades—sent us a beautiful bouquet with a note that read, "As we celebrate our son's wedding today, I will take a moment to remember the love you had for your son, Gary, and the love you still have in his memories."

Friends who are always there, and who remain steadfast through joy, anxieties and grief are among life's rare treasures. They offer quiet understanding and unfailing loyalty. They accept our human weaknesses and care for us despite and because of who we are. They are, across time, our constants in an inconstant world... for better for worse, for richer for poorer, in sickness and health, from PTA to AARP, through raven tresses turned gray and colored blond, through all of life's milestones, and whether or when we are married, widowed, divorced or remarried.

In an honest, abiding friendship, one can always confide without reservation, because "a friend is a person with whom I may be sincere. Before him I may think aloud."[1] Yet even friendships deemed indispensable do not always endure. Some are simply temporary by nature. They fill a given need during a given time, then the laws of in-common and proximity kick in: neighbors move and find they're essentially strangers; colleagues find little to say outside of the workplace; singles get married and marrieds get single; and "Trails end, and companies of men fall apart."[2] Women part company, too... and innately transitory friendships fondly take their place in personal histories. They also become names that time often erases from an address book, a Christmas card list and even conscious thought.

Then there are friendships which dissolve, not through change of venue, but through changes in mind and heart. Human relations are subject to human frailty; thus, as lives and needs and commitments follow different paths, some kinships become unworkable over the long haul. People react to the hazards of living in a variety of ways, not all of them desirable. Some get hung up at the control panel, trying to renovate every one around them. Others become incapable of seeing beyond themselves... never mind feeling empathy with anyone else's joys and trials.

Yet do life experiences really change people, or do they simply intensify true colors? When Rhett longingly told Scarlett in *Gone With The Wind* that he'd liked to think of her as "...a little girl again, before the war and poverty had done things to you..." the implication was, had life been different, Scarlett might have been, too. But would she? Aside from there being no story and that Rhett's character actually knew better, was it war and poverty that made Scarlett headstrong, insensitive and "... so brutal to those who love you... you take their love and hold it over their heads like a whip..." or was she that way by nature?

In fiction or non-, this type of speculation is up for grabs, yet one thing is fact: faced with life's persistent challenges, some people grow. Others stagnate. Some rise to any occasion... and pick up and go on if they fail. Others fall flat on their faces... and stay there. Some gain insight and compassion. Others get self absorbed and melancholy. Still others get hotheaded and mean. And/or any combination thereof.

Not all relationships can overcome these changes. Nor are they meant to. Apart from 'who needs a meanie hothead,' friendships that weather time and circumstance are blessed with intangible, peerless qualities as well as some viable, palpable ingredients... the principal one being that each sincerely wishes the other one well. Intrinsic to such well-wishing—and longevity—neither friend attempts to remake the other to fill his/her own needs. Neither projects personal shortcomings onto the other. Nor sits in judgment. Nor tramples boundaries. And both comfortably bridge the gap between who they once were and who they are today.

Which brings us back to for 'better for worse'... and that makes sense. Common themes define all relationships that are meant to be durable. Long term friendship, like long term love and marriage, thrives not only on shared history and mutual well-wishing, but also by respecting and finding joy in the present.

Common themes also define relationships that cannot work. Brooding about, dwelling in or regurgitating the past, for example, is a surefire way to push any kinship to the brink. Rememberances, yes. Clarifying old misunderstandings, yes... once and for all. But getting mired in all of this? Oh, please! My friend Mary vowed never again after an old acquaintance named Sara kept reminding her and every one in earshot how grateful she should be because Sara had been a good baby-sitter. Considering that the baby in question had just turned forty, the subject was tiresome to say the least. At the same reunion, Sara also kept insisting that Mary justify innocuous, long forgotten and historically rewritten events. And every time Sara lit up another cigarette, she'd upbraid Mary with, "Well, *you* used to smoke." PS: Mary'd quit over twenty years ago.

Cigarettes weren't the issue. They just provided a convenient smoke screen. Inherently flawed relationships frequently consist of one party seeking to vindicate or reinforce his/her shortcomings at the expense of the other. The slogan *friends don't let friends drive drunk* is wonderful sentiment, but in reality it should begin with the word *true.* In true friendship, caring always overrides self interest. But too often alcoholics seek drinking buddies and ridicule 'friends' who stay sober. Foodaholics looking for eating buddies shove food at and otherwise try to undermine their weight conscious 'friends.' And smokers lurk with baited, smelly breath, watching for 'friends' who've successfully quit to light up in a moment of weakness.

Inherently flawed relationships are not forged for sound and legitimate reasons. Apart from the buddy seekers, or scorekeepers who mistake friendship for indentured servitude, there are those who, regardless of age or life status, never outgrow their schoolyard mentality and its definition of the word friend. Yes, they actively seek companionship and/or can masquerade as a sidekick, but they 'befriend' those they perceive as less attractive in order to make themselves look good. Or who they regard as more attractive in order to hang on their coattails. Or those they see as stronger to hide their own weaknesses, or weaker—or in some kind of predicament—to make themselves feel powerful and/or needed. I've met a few across the years... and admit to having been fooled on a couple of occasions. I also recall—from my single days—the pathetic example of women thirty, forty and fifty-plus who'd stab any proclaimed best friend in the back when it came to a guy.

We tell the kids that learning to cope with schoolyard disappointments and betrayals helps them grow. But whether from a classmate or a mental-child-in-adult-clothing, friendships laden with hidden agendas and their resultant disloyalties have no redeeming qualities. Thus, if innately transitory relationships evolve into names which time and circumstance erase, inherently flawed friendships turn into names which we consciously erase with an irate, disillusioned or sometimes gleeful hand.

They also become object lessons. People of good will share a strong tendency to want to believe in the value of every kinship, but one sided well-wishing is not enough. There is an equally strong predisposition to hang onto what was; but friendships, like people, cannot go backwards and cannot be made into what they are not. The Class of Whenever's get together, where Mr. Most Likely to Succeed has become an out-and-out jerk, is the classic bittersweet illustration that some things are best remembered the way they were. So is the story of 'Doris.'

Before Susan moved to a distant state, Doris was her trusted friend and confidante. Or so Sue thought. Doris encouraged her to leave an abusive marriage, was her cheerleader through a difficult divorce and "If I had never seen her again, I'd remember her with great fondness. As it is... " Sue made a helpless gesture with her hands as she recounted the story.

They saw each other again after a seven-year hiatus. Evading Sue's outstretched arms, Doris instead pinched Sue's size ten hips hard and declared she'd gotten fat. That was her first act upon getting off the plane. Her second was to inspect Sue's Little Leaguer whom she'd last seen as a toddler, then remark that the kid looked pathetically thin and undernourished. When they were loading Doris' luggage into the car, the guest wondered out loud if her hostess was moonlighting on street corners to afford such good looking wheels. And when they arrived at Sue's home, Doris protested, "I could picture you in one or two rooms, but not a whole house!"

Things went downhill from there. Doris seemed beside herself that Sue and her family were thriving. She carped, criticized and even stuck her nose in a closet, sniffing, "I remember when you used to dress in rags." Sue shakes her head in disbelief. "It's not that I was denying the past, but she kept rewriting it… I never wore rags! And if I tried to talk about the present, like about my job or how the kids were doing, she'd cut me off in mid sentence." There was immense relief when Doris ran out of insults, went home and was never heard from again. With more pity than disgust—it's been a while—Sue concludes, "I'd known her during a very difficult time. Obviously, she'd gotten off on my bad stuff and couldn't stand for things to be okay."

Doris may have been less subtle, less civilized and more obnoxious than most, but people with similar agendas are not uncommon. Popular thought zeroes in on fair weather friends, those shallow folk who disappear when adversity strikes; but the Dorises of the world are foul weather friends, their polar opposite. No one could ask for more concern and attention than foul weather friends supply during times of sorrow or high drama. But when their concernee's situation improves, foulers feel no joy. On the contrary they feel threatened and even betrayed, and they'll go to great lengths to undermine the present in order to resurrect the good old days when the other person—true or false—could not have survived without them.

You owe me is the credo of the foul weather friend. *You owe me and I'm entitled to your undying gratitude.* Perhaps Doris and her ilk love power trips. Or are just not nice. But, more likely, they either can only feel worthwhile if others are in desperate straits or they are so inwardly miserable they cannot stand to see another person happy. In any event, foul weather friends shatter the primary and most basic rule of enduring relationships: they do not wish the other person well.

Fair weather friends are no great shakes either. Yet both

types can be difficult to spot until a relationship has hit for the cycle. It would be absurd to predict that one's fun loving friends would abandon ship in a crisis... and throw you off the lifeboat to boot. Just as it would be ungracious and paranoid to mistrust the motives of anyone who offers a hand during troubled times. Some things just have to play themselves out. So perhaps friendships are a true reflection of what Forrest Gump said about life... *like a box of chocolates, you never know what you're gonna get.*

And sometimes you get lucky. We share our lives innumerable times across the years, but quality friendships cannot be manufactured. One can make a conscious effort to seek out 'true' friends, especially in new situations or when one's life is in transition. But relationships that thrive on mutual interest, understanding, laughter, encouragement, comfort, counsel and caring do not come along every day. When they do happen—when, once in a while, we are in the right place at the right time—they offer an enriching, rewarding solidarity to our lives and the joy of having someone to bounce ideas off of.

That is especially true of long-time, continual friendships. It also rings true in cyclic relationships which pick up as if their latest chat took place yesterday instead of last year... although the idea bouncing can be a bit different. The enrichment is also part of acquaintanceships that are meant to share our journey down a limited stretch of road. For as long as there is well-wishing, the temporary nature of a friendship does not devalue its significance. Some things just have their place and time; so, if a transitory crossroads is reached, the key is to accept the inevitable, then lock the good in memory and let nature take its course.

One also has to accept the inevitable when, as with Sara or Doris, a relationship no longer holds mutual good will. Regardless of past affections or well-wishes, some Auld Acquaintances really should be forgot. 'Old times sake' is not a license to cross lines where one should never go. And while friendship is rooted in accepting the other person as exactly as he/she is, blanket acceptance does not include accepting abuse. Nor does familiarity bestow upon anyone the right to dispense it. If that crossroads is reached, it's probably best to kick the horse hard and gallop away as fast as its legs can carry you.

A genuine friendship can be compared to feelings of home, a sanctuary where one is always welcome. In *The Brook Kerith,* George Moore notes, "A man travels the world over in search of what he needs and returns home to find it." Certainly that is what one finds in a true friend... and both sides of that analogy were evident to me during a nostalgic trip through New England.

Crossing the bridge over Cape Cod Canal not only brought back memories of my own childhood, but memories of the summer my two oldest boys were five and three. Joan, whose sons were also five and three, and I shared a beachhouse in Harwichport. No, we weren't entirely nuts; we brought along a teenage baby sitter to help out. I remembered the sun and the sand and how Joan and I laughed and got silly and got lost looking for the Mid Cape Highway and how we two young mothers stayed up long after our children were asleep, sharing confidences and talking the night away like coeds in a college dorm.

The following week—or thirty years later, depending on your time frame—Joan and I stayed up again. This time, at her home in Vermont, it was our husbands who were asleep as we remembered that long ago sun and sand and how we laughed and got silly and got lost. We also talked the night away about the little boys who were now grown men, about grandchildren, and our travels, our studies, our careers, whatever. Across the decades, the continent, and a relationship kept alive via letters, phone calls, and only a couple of visits, everything in our lives was different... yet the quality of our friendship had not changed at all.

That visit home brought other changes, however. I always had the fantasy of revisiting the house where I grew up. Of perhaps ringing the doorbell, being invited inside and even seeing my old room. Well, my husband and I found the house all right. But only after driving through a neighborhood so deteriorated that I was in a state of shock. I know change is inevitable, but store fronts along the tree lined boulevard were either boarded up or covered with graffiti or both. My Junior High also looked bigger than I remembered because the buildings around it were in varying stages of crumbling decay. And when we turned onto the street where I grew up, the well kept houses and yards I recalled looked as if they hadn't seen a coat of paint or a lawn mower in the forty years since I'd left for college.

As we pulled up in front of the house, I remembered all the kids I'd known on this once pleasant—now ominous—street. I was also riveted to the spot, which was probably a good thing because getting out of the car seemed like a particularly stupid idea.

And yet… and yet… there was a family who'd lived next door. They had a son my age and a daughter a couple of years younger. I spent a lot of time in their house as a child. I also spent countless hours hanging upside down from a tree branch while the boy and I had spitting contests with cherry pits. Eventually they moved and we all went separate ways. But later, by sheer coincidence, their cousin Lois ended up as my neighbor in a different city and her daughter and my son were even classmates. Small world.

Lois and I have kept in touch across the miles and years; and through her, my tree-climbing buddy Jerry and I have kept apprised of each other's lives. Would we have much in common if everyone was close at hand? Who knows? But I do know one thing. From across the continent, he and his wife cared deeply enough to write a heartwarming, very comforting note when my son died. And though neither had ever met him, they also made a generous contribution in his memory… in memory of the child of a child an old friend knew and cared about long ago.

So perhaps Thomas Wolfe is both right and wrong when he says *You Can't Go Home Again.* Neighborhoods deteriorate. Everything and everyone changes. Yet when home also includes genuine well-wishing that transcends both time and space… you really never have left.

✍

1. Ralph Waldo Emerson

2. Centennial. James Mitchener

Juris—
Imprudence

They have no lawyers among them (in Utopia) for they consider them the sort of people whose profession it is to disguise matters...

—Thomas More, Utopia

When I received the call-up for jury duty, I was willing—if not anxious—to serve. By the time I was excused via peremptory challenge, I wanted to bolt from the courtroom shrieking, "Free at last! Free at last!" I also wanted to de-register myself as a voter and, paraphrasing Scarlett O'Hara in the radish patch vow, *As God is my witness, I'll never do jury again.*

There is nothing more disheartening than viewing law's disorder from the inside out. In his book, *Guilty: The Collapse of Criminal Justice,* the late Judge Harold Rothwax dubbed the Criminal courts, "... a carefully crafted maze, constructed of elaborate and impenetrable barriers to the truth."[1] This jury stint upheld my conviction the Civil courts are no better. That in fact, Judge Rothwax's further indictment, "There is no respect for the truth, and without truth, there can be no justice."[2] is interchangeable between both systems.

It all began with a summons. A piece of paper instructing me to call after Friday of one week but prior to Monday of the next, and foretelling dire consequences if I neglected to do so. I'd been jury-summoned before, but my designated number had always been excused via phone. This time, my number came up.

The assigned call-in hours turned into a weekend of busy signals and unanswered rings. Late Sunday, I finally reached recorded instructions to phone back the next morning between ten and eleven. On Monday, after I'd hit redial for over an hour, another recording ordered me to appear at one o'clock sharp. I complied, received a group number and cooled my heels in a jam-packed assembly room for the rest of the afternoon. Second day, same scenario. Except the heel-cooling was only two hours and ten minutes... at which time a crackling loud speaker ordered my assigned group to report upstairs. Note in passing—overseas travelers and candidates for jury duty or outpatient surgery should follow the same advice: wear loose, comfortable clothing and bring along something to read.

A deputy herded seventy of us into a courtroom. Two attorneys and their jury consultants stood ogling We-the-Possibles as if the group was on display in a singles' bar. Everyone rose as the judge entered. Then everyone sat down. She thanked us for being good citizens and asked that we stand again to take the oath. We stood. Swore. Retook our seats... at which time the judge informed us the pending trial would take three-plus weeks. Therefore, she continued, in order to streamline jury selection, we were to take the multi-page questionnaire both attorneys were handing out, go back down to the assembly room, fill out the query and bring it back up to the courtroom. After that, we were excused for the day.

The questionnaire read like a combined rerun of the McCarthy hearings and Deep Throat. It took more than an hour to fill out. Containing over one-hundred-thirty interrogatives, the query demanded explicit details of our experience with pornography, sexual assault, spousal abuse and etc. It also included inflammatory statement-questions: *Do you believe African Americans are discriminated against... if yes, explain why. Do you believe pornography incites violence against women... if yes, explain yourself. Are you now or have you, any friend, or any member of your family ever been a member of or contributed to organizations concerned with women's rights?* I left the courthouse feeling uneasy.

Back in the juror's assembly room promptly at nine the next morning, we waited only ninety minutes before recall to the courtroom. We were then informed the case in question was considered a Civil—as opposed to Criminal—matter. Since the complaint alleged sexual harassment and discrimination in a seriously dysfunctional workplace, the term 'civil' seemed like an oxymoron.

The plaintiff was a young, black woman who had been raped on the job by a co-worker. The defendants, her ex-employers, had apparently ignored the warning signs, then mouthed sympathy but disavowed accountability... so she sued. The judge, as well as attorneys for both sides, lectured We-the-Possibles about a juror's need to be fair and impartial. At that juncture, I felt perfectly willing and able to do so; however, what followed made it virtually impossible.

For the next two days, I heard 'keeping an open mind' repeatedly defined as (1) denying the existence of race-and-sexism (2) believing bad things happen only to women who 'ask for it' (3) discarding all notions of what comprises a safe, reasonable work environment, and (4) accepting the premise that corporations and individuals are created equal. Pardon my naiveté, but I thought keeping an open mind was different from having a frontal lobotomy.

I also thought a lawyer's need to make a good impression on jurors was crucial. Naive again. Courtroom civility is apparently reserved for sitting juries... those who actually deliberate, reach verdicts and award damages. Potential juries are a distinctly separate matter.

Potentials are an oversized pool of random prospects from which lawyers must pluck twelve 'exemplary' jurors and a couple of alternates. This means draining the pool of any likely juror whose race, ethnicity, life-experience or analytical skills could conceivably obstruct justice or, more to the point, get in the way of winning.

This particular case also dictated identifying and retaining likely jurors who seemed oblivious to racial and gender tensions in the workplace.

Yet no matter how adept a lawyer's selection skills nor how skilled his/her ability to baffle 'em with bullshit, an ideal jury is a fantasy. There is simply no foolproof way to predict how any group is going to react. The best attorneys can do is try to stack things in their client's favor and hope, according to Judge Rothwax, "... you end up with a jury that can be manipulated to accept innuendo as evidence."[3]

Deplorably, this turns jury selection into an adversarial procedure and potential jurors into fair game. Which brings us back to our group of gullibles—I among them—who expected to be treated with dignity.

We answered the voluminous query as honestly and completely as possible. In theory, it was the right thing to do. In reality, we should have been given Miranda warnings... what we said was definitely held against us. In theory, the query was also supposed to save time. In reality, those of us called to the jury box were bombarded with hours of identical questions by attorneys from both sides. Worse still, in lieu of it being used to weed out chancy jurors, it was turned into an assault weapon.

Defendant's counsel gleaned information from the queries, then ambushed selected Possibles with their own responses. When I first realized what was happening, I was baffled. Why were captive citizens, guilty only of answering a summons, undergoing credibility attacks and cross-examination like accused criminals or hostile witnesses? And how could she be so contentious towards jurors who might decide her case? From my vantage point of forced observation, however, her reasons became very clear. Once certain jurors were identified as mismatched or inappropriate, and therefore dispensable, their good will became dispensable as well. But they could still serve this lawyer's purpose. While she went after pre-excused jurors like a pit bull, her jury consultant scrutinized Still-Possibles for their reaction. Nothing personal. Just another way to purify the pool.

As long as she was at it, the same attorney usurped query data to build up and argue her case. For example, several jurors reported having undergone therapy. She applied their collective experience to hammer home two points (1) Help is available during times of emotional stress, and (2) People seek help if they need it. Somehow, information that the plaintiff sought no rape counseling—or any counseling at all—until after she'd filed suit, sneaked its way into this dialogue. The plaintiff was also said to have been suicidal. These shocking revelations were followed by the lawyer's self-satisfied syllogism: Since those who need help seek it, then those who don't seek it don't need it... and therefore cannot be hurting much.

How dare you? I wanted to jump from my seat and scream. *Those who need help the most often don't realize it, resist looking for it or haven't the foggiest idea how to ask for it... that's part of their pain!* It was one of many times during this ordeal that I had to grit my teeth and keep quiet, or risk being cited for contempt.

It was also one of several times I wondered why this attorney wasn't herself cited for contempt. Arguing one's case during jury selection is clearly improper, and the counseling bit was only one example. Another dealt with pornography and nudie pictures on workplace walls. This time, instead of behaving like an attack dog, Ms. Lawyer gushed like a fifties' prom queen, "Do you think men should be forced to alter their work environment just because a woman becomes employed?" Pronouncing 'men' with adoration and 'woman' with disdain, she applied the same coy, breathy approach to her next question: "Should men have to part with personal items such as posters just because a woman finds them offensive?"

It was stipulated the plaintiff had been raped. Yet, instead of trying to mitigate her client's responsibility, this counsel was clearly attempting to justify what happened by rewriting legal precedent. The term sexual harassment not only covers unwelcome overtures and touching, it includes a hostile work environment. That means such things as posters of nude women. It also means pornographic videos, which the plaintiff charged she was subjected to as well.

The young woman had taken a secretarial job at a leasing corporation. It turned out they leased a chain of hotels whose rooms-by-the-hour included XXX flicks. O.K., fine. To each his own. What was not fine, however, was this lawyer's stating that, although the rapist's cubicle was overripe with nudie posters and, as 'part of his job,' he checked out porn videos within the plaintiff's hearing and peripheral vision, the lady had no right to object... neither to the decor nor his decorum.

The wisest approach to dealing with sexual harassment is prevention. Defendant's attorney preferred the time-honored method of blaming and demonizing the victim. Requesting that a man remove his girlie posters hardly equates a woman with Lorena Bobbitt; yet, that is exactly how defendant's counsel made it sound. And by acting herself like a sappy, wide-eyed innocent, counsel implied that no respectable lady—like her—would ever interfere with a man's work, dare suggest he clean up his act... or get raped.

We were still in jury selection, by the way. Was this arguing a case or what?

Against my will, this lawyer also manipulated me to her advantage. There is and was absolutely no connection between my having divorced an abusive husband twenty-five years earlier and this plaintiff's complaint against her employers; yet, defendant's counsel invented one. "You were a battered wife, but you left, isn't that true? I mean, you were in a bad situation, but you got out of it, isn't that true? You even had small children, and you knew things wouldn't be easy, but you took them and got away, isn't that true?" Then, clearing her throat, she concluded smugly, "So you agree women don't stay in any situation they don't want to!"

No! No! No! Of course it was true that I left. But I had a place to go, not everyone does. It is also true I've stayed in horrendous work environments because of survival. *How dare you twist my life's ancient history to imply this woman wasn't really upset by her surroundings?* I wanted to protest. *People can become emotionally paralyzed in terrifying situations. Being afraid she had no choice doesn't mean this woman liked it, or encouraged it, or stayed—and perhaps even invited the rape—in order to cash in on it.* I could, however, express none of these sentiments. The lawyer cut me off after 'yes' or 'no.'

As a potential juror, I had divulged personal facts in good faith. By what legal justification did this attorney then usurp those facts to make me her unwitting witness? And why was she allowed to case-build by expropriating data from jury questionnaires in the first place? Was the subtlety of her maneuvers lost on the judge? Was the judge asleep or too jaded to care? Was the plaintiff's attorney too intimidated or inept to object? Was the defendant's lawyer just close enough to the line not to get called on her behavior? Whatever the explanation, the entire scene was a travesty.

At the end of selection day one, the judge asked We-the-Possibles if anyone really wanted to serve on this jury. No one replied. It was a rare, welcome moment of comic relief. Most of what transpired in that courtroom, however, lacked any redeeming feature. The defendant's attorney confronted a thirty-something man. "So..." long, dramatic pause, "your mother was a member of N.O.W?" Looking startled, the man replied, "Yes." "Has this affected your thinking? Would it get in the way of being fair and impartial?" This time the guy shrugged, "No." Counsel turned, retreated a couple of steps, then whirled back and—in a voice that dripped sarcasm—demanded, "How old is your mother?" "Fifty-three." The attorney then spit out each syllable with all deliberate slowness, "F i f t y - t h r e e?" She pretended to be amazed. "Definitely a woman before her time!"

Now it was my turn to be amazed. *Pardon me, but your ignorance is showing, lady. That was our time.* Once again, I wanted to jump from my seat, this time to grab the lawyer's arrogant shoulders and shout, *women of our generation opened opportunity's doors for women of yours... so that today, in this courtroom, you can be an attorney and I can feel like I helped create a Frankenstein.* Unfortunately, she is not the only Frankenstein around... and I am not even certain which type she is.

Is this attorney a power-hungry hater who gets her jollies from attacking others? Does she feel compelled to abuse people... or is her courtroom demeanor all an act? Instead, does she equate power with being male, fear that acknowledging other women's value diminishes her own, and disparage other females to be 'one of the boys?' Since only clerical jobs were open to Supreme Court Justice Sandra Day O'Connor when Her Honor first graduated law school, does this attorney's knowledge of such relatively recent history convince her she must do anything—to anyone—to prove herself? Or am I giving her too much credit? Perhaps she exists in a vacuum, feels totally divorced from earlier generation's struggles and arrogantly believes those efforts are irrelevant because she would have made it anyway. Maybe she would have, but glossing over women's collective past and continuing struggles does not mean this attorney can avoid their consequences, no matter how much she tries to blame the victim. And speaking of blaming the victim, does this lawyer prissily, piously believe only women who send out inviting signals are sexually harassed? Has she honestly never experienced gender discrimination? Would she recognize sexual harassment if it came up and pinched her on the butt?

On the other hand, if this attorney is none of the above, and/or understands all of the above, and was just protecting the interests of her client, what does that say about the ethics she has had to adopt? More important, what does that say about her profession? Must representing a client equate to bloodsport? Must courtrooms resemble a quagmire of Orwellian doublespeak? Why is it O.K. to attack innocent or obviously truthful people's credibility just because it gets in your way? Why is it O.K. to replace honesty with cold-blooded strategy, civility with intimidation, and leave those who've experienced the inner workings of the system feeling wounded and/or deeply distrustful? Is there no shame? And is it any wonder that hate-lawyer jokes are so universally popular?

In the quiet sanctity of my car, I sat pondering many things. I thought about the sitting jury… preempted of all minorities as well as anyone who seemed sensitive to gender-based bias. Then again, they seemed like a nice group who would try their best, no matter how their composition had been tampered with. I also thought about the plaintiff's attorney. He'd come across as no match for his opponent, but perhaps he'd been saving his big guns for when they'd count. Most of all, my heart went out to the plaintiff. She'd already been raped at work and now seemed about to be raped by the courts.

Regardless of how solid or weak her case turned out to be, or how weak or valid the defendants', what had taken place during selection was nothing compared to what was coming. How would this young woman stand up as a witness, I wondered. How would she endure deliberate, malicious twisting of her words, trashing of her character, the witchhunt that would define her past, the sneering, humiliation and the merciless attempts to shatter her life? No matter what the outcome, even if the jury rewarded her handsomely for her suffering, the cost of winning would be a nightmare. Losing would be even worse. Relieved not to have to be part of this, I turned the key in the ignition and headed home.

✍

1. We're In the fight of our lives. Parade Magazine. July 28, 1996

2. ibid.

3. ibid.

Help! I'm Being Held Prisoner

Political Correctness—The Ghetto of the Mind

Much of my father's life was spent in search of an elusive destination. He was not on some deep-meaning spiritual quest, however. The reason was far less complicated. Dad had absolutely no sense of direction. More times than I can remember, he would lose his way pulling out of the driveway or turn left instead of right just going around the block. And when he died, the hearse took the wrong exit off the freeway and got lost on its way to the cemetery.

Some of us thought that was funny... although a distant cousin was offended by our chuckles. Yet those who loved my father most knew how he'd have relished the irony; and that, in spite of the sadness of the day, we were sharing his last laugh.

If one is lucky, his/her life is enriched by words of wisdom which pass from generation to generation. Mine came from my father: "No matter what ever happens, no matter what life brings, never lose your sense of humor." Dad's legacy was to appreciate that humor celebrates life. That it brings together the discordant like a harmony of the heart. That humor makes the worst of times bearable, pinpoints life's absurdities and unmasks the foibles of the human condition. And most important of all, that humor helps us form a mutual bond... if only we let it.

I have long celebrated the philosophy and wisdom of the man who really did get lost on the way to his own funeral. More than thirty years down the road, however, I fear his lessons are on their own way to turning up missing.

We have become a culture under siege. A nation surrounded by self-imposed, invisible ghettos. With suspicion as their cornerstones and disapproval their pillars, these modern-day medieval confines block out the truth of diversity, the light of laughter and all presumption of good-will. Smile not. Joke not. Choose every word carefully. Somewhere, somehow, someone is bound to be offended.

Escape is not easy from the ghettos of the mind. All exits are zealously guarded. On the extreme right we have the righteous... those who claim a direct, inflexible line to God. These righteous declare it demonic, heretical and un-American-to-the-point-of-treason not to share their beliefs; hence, they feel wholly (or holy) justified to decree how the entire nation should think, feel, pray and even play... which is allowed so long as nobody except Ken Starr and his ilk mentions sex or otherwise has any fun. In raw quest for political power, they avow censorship and disavow separation of church and state—as long as it's their church—and blithely resort to rumor and innuendo if it furthers their agenda. They also seem determined to keep women barefoot, pregnant... and definitely in their place.

Defending the left are the equally self-righteous Politically Correct. PCs do not claim heaven among their MCI Friends and Family. Instead, they unilaterally anoint *themselves* as guardians of what is acceptable. Political correctness also foregoes accusations of heresy; however, its agenda is no less hell-bent on sanitizing the universe to a dull monotony of sameness. Their single-mindedness and myopia make me wonder if Kurt Vonnegut somehow foresaw it all when he wrote about a place where the handsome were masked, the graceful bogged down with weights and the intelligent shackled by ringing bells to make them lose track of their thoughts.

The Politically Correct insist they are different from—even morally superior to—the righteous, whom they fault for claiming moral superiority. After all, PCs insist you will agree that political correctness disavows discrimination, harassment and censorship. At the same time, those who consider themselves politically correct condemn and censor at will. Any person who fails to meet their unilaterally-imposed language standards is chastised as insensitive or denounced as whatever type bigot can be made to fit. Silly old standbys like "a rabbi and a priest were comparing notes..." are anti-Semitic or anti-Church. Citing demographics, ethnicity, skin color or the need to limit population growth is racist. And, with the glaring exception of anything Bobbitt, differentiating between men and women smacks of sexism, misogyny and/or homophobia.

"You can paint yourself into a corner," my husband suggested when I was thinking out loud about this article. "How are you going defend what sounds like race or sexist slurs?" But my intention is not to promote language which fosters oppression or any disgusting 'ism.' I am defending our right to laugh as a method of coping and our wisdom to know the difference.

They told Yeltsin jokes in the bread lines of newly-democratic Russia. Still do. It helps pass the time even if it doesn't take away the hunger pangs. In yesteryear's Soviet Union, folks told government jokes, too... very quietly... very judiciously. In this country, poverty quips are shared in food-stamp lines and jobless jokes in the unemployment office. And whenever there is a disaster, parodies begin before the news flashes end.

Aside from that, Mrs. Lincoln, how did you enjoy the play? Aside from that, Mrs. Kennedy, how did you enjoy the motorcade? Christa McAuliff was a civics teacher... now she's history. Gross bad taste? Absolutely! Mean spirited? Not necessarily. Over the years, I have heard all sorts of irreverent, improper remarks from perfectly reverent, proper people. Laughter is the great healer. It helps to make the unbearable bearable. Those who lack the ability to understand that are sensitivity challenged. Or is that "tactile-ly impaired?

Of course tragedy and grave adversity is not funny. But if humor helps to make the tragic tolerable, so be it. Of course the fight for human rights is not funny. Neither is it automatically harmed by asking *how many Norwegians it takes to change a light bulb.*

Nor is it heresy to observe the comic side of organized—or disorganized—religion. Granted, freedom is imperiled when zealots attempt to dismantle separation of church and state. Granted, all are at risk when any religion is hell bent on imposing its beliefs via legislation… or advocates shooting doctors in cold blood. These are concepts which jeopardize both life and basic rights. A sense of the absurd does not. What a shame, for example, if the eternal rabbi, priest and minister are forced to decide, "We have to stop meeting like this." Or heavenly newcomers can no longer be told that yonder walled-off area is strictly for the (fill in the blank)s because "they think they're the only ones here." You know you're in trouble when… you cannot see the fundamental humor of countless religions claiming ownership of sole, universal Truth.

When my children were in their teens, two of their friends had Confirmations in the same weekend. So Friday evening we went to the synagogue and Sunday to a Lutheran church. What with the blessings and the laying on of hands, the services were remarkably similar. So were the receptions which followed. Both featured a white cake frosted with blue roses congratulating the confirmation class. In fact, the only apparent difference seemed the Cross on one cake and Star of David on the other… prompting my fourteen-year-old to observe "I hope the good Lord has a sense of humor."

I believe she does. Or he does. Or he/she does. I also agree with the late comedian, Henry Morgan, who concluded his autobiography with, "If it is true that God created man, by now he surely has laughed himself to death." Yet poking fun at any form of dogma, belief or configuration of the Almighty automatically condemns one in the rigidity of today. On the right, you're a heretic. On the left, a bigot.

Perhaps bigotry itself is in the eye of the beholder. Morgan would probably be amused to find himself quoted on the same page as Oliver Wendell Holmes; yet it seems to fit. Justice Holmes noted, "The mind of the bigot is like the pupil of the eye; the more light you pour on it, the more it will contract." I am certain he meant the left eye as well as the right. Just because one is intolerant or inflexible does not mean he/she is correct. Politically or otherwise.

It all comes down to, 'is the message received really the one being sent?' Is there mal-intent or in fact any intent at all besides having fun? From Gilbert and Sullivan to Tom Lehrer, parody has spanned the generations. Jabbing out equally to the left and the right, it has made us laugh at all things personal and political. Lehrer incidentally, claiming life had out-satirized itself, stopped writing farce when Henry Kissinger received the Nobel Peace Prize... If only he'd waited a couple of decades, Lehrer could have finally thrown in the towel when, during the early days of Lewinskygate, convicted Watergate burglar G. Gordon Liddy intoned the need for honesty in the Oval Office on CNN.

In spite of guys like Liddy, others of us, neither as brilliant nor well known as Lehrer, refuse to give up. Convinced the serious need not always be taken seriously, my family has joined forces to make fun of just about everything we can think of. As teenagers, my sister and I devised such ditties as an ode to the Senator from Wisconsin, *On McCarthy. On McCarthy... you're sure one good Joe.* Years later, my older kids concocted crazy newscasts like the Humphrey-Brinkley Report, *Good night, Hubert, Good Night David.* And my youngest son parodied Ronald Reagan or Bill Clinton with equal abandon. He could also mimic yiddish, ebonics or any other accent, and his spoof of evangelist Gene Scott—the Reverend 'Green Spot'—was a classic.

Rancor was—or is—rarely intended. The ideas just flow. Gilbert and Sullivan's *I Am the Very Model of a Modern Major General* easily converted to 'I Am the Very Model of a Modern Vegetarian.' Gershwin's *They're Writing Songs of Love, but Not for Me,* to "They're Selling Bathing Suits, but Not for Me (with cellulite, from head down to my feet...)." For the record, revision number one was not meant to deride the carnivorously challenged. Neither was the second meant to slam the size disadvantaged. In fact, if I wrote those lyrics to gibe anybody, it was me.

Parody personifies life's absurdities. It is not going to go away because some unimaginative, non-visionary group now deems it no longer correct. On the other hand, being unafraid to be silly is not the same as dispensing calculated cruelty. Anything which deliberately means to humiliate, hurt or destroy is not funny. The Ku Klux Klan telling race or ethnic jokes is not acceptable. But that scenario itself makes good fodder for the satirist.

So do most things. An ancient sage observed any subject which cannot bear raillery is suspicious. And surviving words of wisdom often contain basic truth... even through countless reinterpretations. Surely I am not the only one who is amused that the Passover seder, an integral part of Jewish tradition, has been reinterpreted so many times is now celebrated at many churches.

Passover commemorates the Exodus, recorded history's first successful fight for freedom from slavery. Noting this at a church-usurped seder, a minister asked her congregation for examples of modern day slavery. Racism was the first response. Followed by sexism and ethnic cleansing. When somebody suggested political correctness, however, the entire room burst into applause.

As an added note, I was on the planning committee for that particular service. Once we had decided who would supply the wine and/or matzo balls and who would—and how to—say the blessings, someone hesitantly offered a story about our 'old friends' the rabbi, minister and priest. Suddenly, everyone was dusting off favorite irreverent stories, laughing at each other's jokes and marveling at how refreshing it was that no one was upset or pointing accusing fingers. That we had to marvel at all was a sad commentary. In an allegedly free society, what an awful price is paid when hyper-sensitivity steamrolls the ability to reason... and category after category is declared 'unjokeworthy' and forcibly relegated to the junk pile.

Political correctness is a form of tyranny. It puts the meanest possible interpretation on everything, accuses everyone of trying to do in everyone else and substitutes a few carefully selected words for the entire English language. Worst of all, its skewed, judgmental perspective annihilates fairness and equality, the very things it is supposed to promote.

Variations exist. Diversity... is. A world where everyone is identical simply cannot be mandated, any more than compassion and tolerance can be created on demand. No matter how loud nor how frequent the PC tantrums, denying those facts will not ensure absolute fairness. And equal opportunity will never be attained through social paranoia, holier-than-thou type blame or making it necessary to obtain a search warrant to find common sense.

Traffic signs which read "Slow—Children" are meant to warn drivers they are in school zones, not to insult the developmentally challenged. An orchestra's performing the classic *Peter and the Wolf* is neither thumbing its nose at endangered species nor encouraging cruelty to animals, and *God Rest Ye Merry Gentlepersons* is a stupid revisionist Christmas carol. Oops! Make that seasonal song.

Of course we need to eliminate the hateful, divisive, insensitive, racist and sexist stuff from our vocabularies as well as our actions. But scolding, shunning, rewriting history or looking for hidden meanings under every rock does nothing to accomplish that end. Of course we need to reach out and promote understanding. But thwarting freedom of expression sabotages that entire sentiment. Humor and pathos are very closely related. If we are to feel one another's pain and even mourn one another's losses, we must be allowed to acknowledge our differences as well as our foibles-in-common. And to celebrate—and even spoof—the totality of who we are.

To those who find that notion fraught with danger, perhaps it is your malice that is showing. And your dull rigidity as well. Try lightening up. Unyielding political correctness manages to piss off potential allies as well as antagonists. Otherwise it accomplishes nothing. The suffering of all the oppressed peoples of the world cannot be eradicated by gagging those who express themselves differently, blindfolding those who can see shades of gray or stifling anyone who appreciates the funny side of life

Easter Week the Whole Year Round

Stop Trampling on My Constitutional Rights

Six years, forty million-plus taxpayer dollars and tons of specious headlines later, the President of the U.S. proved to be excruciatingly human... a sinner instead of a saint. But before the media gloats 'we told you so' and absolves their own sins of trashing a presidency for the sake of sales and Neilsens, please note that the first draft of this chapter was written in 1994. It opened with the following paragraph: Crucify Him! Crucify Him! Jesus was betrayed. Then, blind to injustice and oblivious to judgment of history, the mob worked itself into a frenzy and clamored for His blood. Today, as we approach the new Millennium, the betrayal we witness is that of democracy... by a media-mob blind to integrity, unmindful of history's judgment and with "Crucify" still the watchword of its faith. Too often—and too often obscene—the sole distinction between Calvary and Capitol Hill seems the Biblical crowd's lack of cameras and microphones.

Jesus, of course, was innocent. But this section is about a mob's behavior, not the eventual guilt or innocence of its targets. It is also about the mob-press substituting facts with gossip and partisan hachetwork; inventing crimes, then fashioning a criminal-to-fit.

Glancing backward, we see that from day one of the Clinton presidency, the media reported accusations which deemed the first couple guilty of every heinous felony imaginable... including murder. Finally, the worst—the only—thing that turned up was Bill's fooling around on his wife, then denying it... yes, even under oath. Was the President's dalliance reckless and stupid? Absolutely. His behavior a betrayal of trust? You bet. Was it also asinine and abhorrent? Certainly many would find it so. But unusual? According to statistics, definitely not! He was neither the first president nor first spouse to fall off the fidelity wagon; nor was he the first one to deny it. He was, however, the first president forced to exist under such inhumane and indecent personal scrutiny. While none of that excuses Clinton's conduct, neither do his actions excuse the media—nor any of us—from being hypocrites.

In relative importance, "I did not have sexual relations with that woman..." pales in comparison to most of history's great lies. Yet in order of hypocrisy, the media's daily pious, but orgiastic proclamations that it absolutely *hated* covering all minutiae of the Presidents sex life, may well take the prize. Second place goes to its insistence that under the guise of the public's right to know, we, too, must be privy to and needed to appreciate the intimate details.

Infidelity rocks the foundations of any marriage; thus, any details were Hillary's to know if she felt so inclined and she also had every reason to feel pissed. But, it was no one else's business; for in no way do rolls-in-the-hay rock the foundations of this country—nor do they comprise high crimes or even misdemeanors.

At the same time, the President was the target of high crimes and misdemeanors. A righteous, obsessed Ken Starr proved himself incapable of separating politics from prosecutorial 'devotion.' Aligned with those determined to beat Clinton by scandal, since it couldn't be done in the voting booth, he stalked his prey at the cost of the Constitution. And, smelling blood and seeing dollar signs, the media gleefully abetted all attempts to nullify the electoral process... sacrificing its own credibility in the process.

"In the public's view, the press is no different than Monica," noted William Schneider in the August 16, 1998 *L.A. Times*. "They're all tramps." Possibly that was a bit harsh on Ms. Lewinsky who comes across more like a hormone-driven groupie who talks too much. Yet Schneider, if anything, was too kind to the press. I also believe the Gallup Poll that sparked his comments reflects my premise that—regardless of the President's folly—the media's Monica madness was a logical, predictable outgrowth of all that had gone before.

From 1994 to the final acquittal vote, I found that keeping this chapter current was an exercise in futility. I also found that political examples become archaic before they can be put on paper; hence, if some of my references seem time worn, they are nevertheless timely in their warning that whenever the press surrenders objectivity for sleaze and big bucks, the freedom of every citizen is at risk.

Now, let me reclaim what I can from the original and some rewrites, and let us rewind the tape to the opening days of Clinton's first term. Recall how rumors abounded and how no one—including the dead and how they got that way—was spared. *Vince Foster did not commit suicide. He was Hillary's secret lover. And/or he was murdered to silence his knowledge about notorious crimes.* The atmosphere was so charged, so accusatory, cabinet nominees were headlined as threats to democracy… for stuff like 'nanny crimes' and their equivalent. Back to Capitol/Calvary Hills, one could imagine that if Jesus himself had faced confirmation in early 1993, TV pundits would have focused on His association with a known prostitute… never mind why. 'Reliable sources' would have rumored alcoholism… why else turn water into wine? And healing the sick would have been denounced on hate radio as another clandestine Hillary plot to bring us universal healthcare.

Fast forward to the start of term two. Despite four years of journalists pronouncing that Clinton's presidency was history, Bill renewed his oath of office with popularity ratings rivaling Ronald Reagan's. And Hillary was not, as reporters predicted, in shackles for all her criminal activities, but at his side.

Now roll back the tape to January 1995 and the ascendance of Newt the Speaker… who was greeted as *Newt, Newt, Newt* the Savior and quickly became Newt the sap. His critics insist Mr. Speaker's attitude did him in. But it's hard to be humble if one is being worshiped, even when the adoration stems from in-your-face trashing of the President. Yet Newt should have known better than to believe what he read in the papers. Even though the media initially behaved as if this member of the U.S. Congress was their Divinely chosen Czar, he'd been around long enough to appreciate—first hand—that bloodsport begets better ratings than adulation. He also should have known that, since no public servant belongs on a pedestal to begin with, his popularity plummet was inevitable. For whether or not it was true that Newt's demeanor was arrogant, his Contract With America a shell game and his ethics appalling to the point of severe reprimand and a $300,000 fine, it is unquestionably true that the media giveth and the media taketh away.

The press has become intoxicated with power. Knowing it can make or break anyone, the demands of true democracy—including the holding of those in power accountable—has undergone a perverted evolution. Hence, the First Amendment right to recount and interpret events without fear of retaliation now translates to: whenever reporters tire of a particular leader, long for a juicy story or just plain have it in for someone, truth and straight news become expendable.

Long before Hillary was derided for speaking of a right wing conspiracy and long before Kenneth Starr became Grand Inquisitor, my original draft stated: in the prevailing business climate, amusement, scandal and stimulation (sexy and otherwise) builds communications empires and the technology of instant and round-the-clock communication begets atrocious competition at the cost of integrity. By coincidence or just terrible confluence, in the prevailing societal climate, honest conservative tenets have been seized by a fanatical right willing to stop at nothing—including a jihad—to gain its objective. Therefore, the more the media eschews facts and caters to titillation, the more eagerly the unholy crusade supplies it with blueprints for yellow journalism.

I also wrote that an apparent media rule-of-thumb has become selective accountability… with the media making all the selections. Why, I asked, is it now acceptable to employ and even elicit the words of someone's known detractors to use as source material? Why has it become OK to purposely omit a defamer's possible motives? If the press must hold those in power accountable for everything they do, say or have ever said or done, why are those seeking power excused from similar scrutiny? Especially when the seekers make preposterous, slanderous allegations? And what has happened to confirmation? Why, as long as an accusation makes good headlines, does the media now feel free to react with *break the story now, check for accuracy and agendas later?*

Tabloid journalism was once an aberration but it has now become standard fare; and mudslinging, once viewed as partisan rhetoric, has been perfected to a mainstream artform. If lurid, indiscriminate hyperbole have taken the place of checking one's sources, other rules seem to be: insinuate. Smear. Make irresponsible, historically inaccurate comparisons. And, when all else fails, fall back on sly, mean-spirited innuendo. A 1994 wire service report omitting the reason the President "abruptly canceled" an appearance is a perfect example. His mother died.

Though loathsome, the omission about Virginia Kelley's death was a very minor example. Of greater significance were the relentless, unprecedented efforts to topple a president just for the hell of it—or at least just to beat the competition. Paying cursory attention to program proposals or whether bills had popular support, from day one, the press focused on trashing and trivializing the presidency. Also from the get-go, treatment of the Clinton administration evoked chilling reminders of Cardinal Richelieu's words, "Give me six lines written by the hand of the most honest of men, I will find something in them which will hang him."

The question is why? Simplistic answers include 'who controls the purse strings?' and/or the conservative belief that the White House actually *belongs* to the GOP. Stephen Hess of the Brookings Institution offered another view. According to Hess, there was an unwritten pact among the media to sink this president from the outset; but curiously enough, not because of his politics or his character. Apparently, back in early 1993, Clinton's new press operations team had the audacity to limit reporter access to some areas that had been open during previous administrations. Stated Hess, "The incoming team had not yet learned a basic rule of media management. *An idle reporter is a dangerous reporter.*"[1]

The same *San Francisco Chronicle* editorial which included that quote conceded, "The Washington Press Corps contains some correspondents whose egos far exceed their intelligence or understanding. " It also admitted, "The chances of transmitting a favorable message are diminished when members... are restricted from entering offices... It isn't only that their feelings are hurt, but understandably they become suspicious while confined in enforced idleness."[2]

Understandably? Oh, come on! Is this blaming the victim or what? Boredom, bruised egos and/or sulking rage in no way justifies anyone's attempt—including the media's—to bring down the government.

President Clinton did have one temporary respite during his first six years, however. Priorities are priorities... so DC fervor took a back seat to OJ fever when the press turned its attention to 'the trial'. There too, a crazed pack of reporters pinpointed their larger agenda: sales via sensationalism at any cost. Rather than stress the peril of women whose partners batter or vilify them, it was more titillating to savage Nicole's reputation. And rather than cite statistics which show that domestic battery victims frequently end up dead, they cited experts who said, because of OJ's revered fame and fortune, jurors could pass off beatings and name callings as "well, that's the way couples are."[3] On ABC's *Night Line*, even the esteemed Ted Koppel copped out: "This is not a case about spousal abuse. This is a murder case."

What irony! The press had a captive audience. It could have seized the OJ moment to give life saving information... and raked in ratings and the big bucks to boot. But domestic tranquillity works against the media's best interest. How would they survive without sleaze and violence?

As it is on the homefront, so it is (and was) in the nation's capital. With OJ's trials over, the press turned its attention back to Washington, DC... and found a paucity of new dirt or impending doom. So they sneered, *What kind of place in history will President Clinton have? The economy is sound. He's kept us out of war. What a loser! He'll be remembered like Chester A. Arthur.* Apparently there was no way to please a blood thirsty press who would rather play Peeping Tom. Or pay nostalgic homage to Cardinal Richelieu and his finding something within "... six lines written by... the most honest of men... which will hang him."

Perhaps they were confusing six lines with eighteen minutes of tape. One of Watergate's enduring legacies is that no president since Richard Nixon has been fully trusted. Another is those visions of Pulitzer-plums left dancing in reporters' collective heads. Woodward and Bernstein won the Pulitzer for exposing a well-orchestrated scheme to affect the outcome of an election and obstruct justice to cover it up. True, such scoops do not come along every day. But just as Oval Office whoopie does not equal plotting election nullification, neither does peeking into what is strictly personal—or fabricating major events—justify savaging any president for ratings or cravings for the Pulitzer. Nor will it ever transform mediocre reporters into "Woodstein."

Not that reporters don't try. Erasing eighteen taped minutes helped to do in Richard Nixon's presidency. Nearly two decades later, a skulking press manipulated the teenage Bill Clinton's admiration of another president, John F. Kennedy, by blending Watergate's legacy into Camelot. 'Erasing' all but the words *one hundred days* from JFK's inaugural address, they then charged the newly elected Clinton with the hopeless task of altering the entire direction of the country (if not the world) within the first hundred days of his administration... or be branded a failure.

It was steadily downhill from there; yet JFK never meant his words to portend such irrational demands. He understood that long range societal change could not be accomplished over night... nor *in one hundred days, nor one thousand days nor in our lifetime on this planet.* In fact, what he said was, *'but let us begin.'* Hence, the media's initial focus on Clinton's first one hundred days was either sheer stupidity, sheer story building or sheer cynicism banking on the majority of Americans not being old enough to remember 1960. In any event, in their haste to make headlines, reporters revealed themselves to be as unclear on the quote as they were on the concept. They also flaunted their shameful ignorance about this nation's form of government.

The United States is a democracy with Executive, Legislative and Judicial branches for balance of power. We do not have a parliamentary system where the president outlines an agenda that is automatically rubber stamped… and neither are we supposed to have a fourth branch of government, an extra-constitutional Grand Inquisitor who wields unlimited power and funds and is answerable to no one. Somehow just writing those last three sentences conjures up visions of a junior high civics class rolling its collective eyes and mouthing, "Duh!" And they'd be right. Go back and study Civics 101, all national media. Discover what Congress is supposed to be about. And while you are at it, read *The Rise and Fall of the Third Reich.* Remind yourself what can happen without those checks and balances and how close we came to disaster in the winter of 1998/99. Also remind yourself what can happen when the media gang rapes documents like the Constitution, overlooks their rape by others and/or helps to submerge any nation in hatred. Do you really want to share responsibility for the inevitable outcome?

As it is, you already bear responsibility for putting the public's right to make informed decisions at risk. By sensationalizing and giving weight to every rumor, and by confusing genuine policy and other issues with the Clinton-haters' racy fantasies and distortions, you've helped to create a climate where the serious and the patently absurd hold equal status. And when it is difficult to distinguish the tainted from the truth, both are often dismissed as partisan crap.

I plead guilty to being an anachronism. But I really believe the guarantee of a free press implies an obligation to combine unbiased reporting with thoughtful analysis and commentary… not pandering to the lowest common denominator or selling one's wares for the current equivalent of thirty pieces of silver. Op Ed pages and TV editorials are the appropriate forum for personal bias and varying points of view; but bias blazened in headlines or hidden within non-editorial text is another issue entirely.

No democracy should depend upon its leaders pandering to the media. All holders of elected office should be allowed to be judged on the effectiveness and content of their programs, not by journalistic blackmail. Or, as with recovered memory travesty spelled out in "Toss the Laundry List in the Garbage," the bastardization of Miranda Rights into some sadistic, fool-proof *anything you've ever said and/or done, and anything I declare that you did or I think you may have meant, and even things you did not do but I feel like saying or putting into print that you did... can and will be held against you.* Add this to the media's power to portray lack of evidence as proof of a cover-up and/or anything short of an anguished confession as further proof the accused is lying, and we have new spin on abuse of power: accusers have carte blanche and full immunity while their accused are denied any right of self defense. This is a tenet of fascism. And since the First Amendment cannot exist, never mind survive, under fascism, the free press is literally committing suicide... and dragging us along for the ride.

We the People elect our President. The media have no mandate to make that, or any, selection for us. They are salaried reporters, not our duly elected representatives; and, as a nation, we merit better than to be governed by a junta camouflaged as the free press. We are also entitled to a fair accounting. Again back in 1994, Duke University political scientist, David Barber, noted, "We're moving from a period of impressionism to one of reality... to people wanting... help with jobs and health care and crime... But while Clinton is dealing with reality, the media are mistaking the Presidency for largely trivial matters."[4] Since the press subsequently spun far more out of control than Barber or anyone could have imagined, the time is long overdue for newsmakers to retire their game of *Trivial Pursuit.*

It is also time to adopt some rules of fair play. When *Washington Post* reporter, Janet Cooke, fabricated both an eight-year-old heroin addict and the story of his plight, she was fired and condemned by her colleagues. Although that happened in 1981, Cooke remains persona non grata to this day. But if the media vows never to hire her again, why don't they hold each and every one of themselves to equivalent standards?

Yes, occasionally sacrificial lambs are made of press peers... since the media now seeks respectability via limited 'repentance.' CNN/Time retracted a story about nerve gas being tossed at defectors during the Vietnam War. They even fired producer April Oliver and some cohorts. *The Boston Globe's* Patricia Smith and Mike Barnicle were forced to resign for allegedly conjuring up episodes, quotes and people. But who is fooling whom? In context of the Clinton years, how much greater were Cooke's, Smith's or Barnicle's crimes than *Newsweek's* 1994 anti-Hillary stock trading article that, one day later, was denounced as "false and irresponsible" by its "primary source?" And how much worse was Oliver's crime than those of her colleagues who gleefully rushed to print or airtime quoting dubious, unchecked sources? At least Cooke later returned her 1981 Pulitzer. But what about editors who bury retractions in places least likely to be seen? Or who, for example, when the president defended his wife's integrity after the *Newsweek* story, sneer back in headlines, "She Is Not A Crook"?

For those who've forgotten or are too young to remember, 'Not a Crook' is a cynical—if not diabolical—likening to Nixon and Watergate. Hence, one more time, while it was—and is—completely irrelevant, in this instance, as long as it served a press corps agenda, 'Watergate lives.' Tragically, Vincent Foster does not. Yet even after the DC police, the FBI and alas, even Starr himself confirmed that Foster's death was a suicide, where were the media's apologies for spreading those barbarous rumors? Once again, how much greater was Ms. Cooke's crime?

The phrase 'at the mercy of the media' is an oxymoron. No one is safe; but Presidents, First Ladies and other public figures are especially vulnerable. In the classic syndrome of confronting those who thrive on cruelty, there is no way one can defend him/herself without inviting more of the same. Private citizens like the accused-and-later-exonerated Olympic bomber, Richard Jewell, or Khalid Khawar who was standing next to Senator Robert F. Kennedy the night he was shot, have an outside chance of redress… provided they are willing to go through more agony and chance ending up with but a Pyrrhic victory. A supermarket tabloid, *The Globe,* printed a conspiracy theory depicting Khawar, not Sirhan Sirhan, as RFK's true assassin. Khawar sued and a Los Angeles County jury awarded him $1.1 million in damages. But he's yet to collect. Although the story proved totally false, *The*

Globe is appealing via First Amendment... claiming freedom of the press means the right to destroy innocent lives. Worse still, the 'mainstream' media is cheering on its tabloid cohort.

Before I knew Khawar's victory was hollow, I cheered for both that jury and for a man gutsy enough to take on the press... and win. I also thought back to RFK's assassination. Whether Bobby Kennedy could have helped us find that better world he urged us to seek is not possible to know. What I do know is, the morning after he was shot, I held my nine-year-old son in my arms wondering, "What can I say to him? This is the third time he's had to witness something like this. How can he... how can any of these kids grow up believing in anything?" From a vantage point approaching three decades, my fears seem to have been well grounded.

The three assassins' bullets murdered more than a president, a presidential candidate and a modern-day Moses. They wiped out messages of hope and a sense of possibility for the upcoming generation. How could parents reasonably tell children who'd seen beloved leaders shot before their eyes that those men's lives had meaning, or that wrongs-can-be-righted and one-person-can-make-a-difference? How could they advocate putting faith in democracy's principles when, in quick succession, the kids then saw a nation turned on its head by an ill-advised, star-crossed war and a subsequent president exposed as a crook and obstructer-of-justice? Oh, adults could mouth hopeful words all right, and even mean them; but when an entire generation's convictions are defined by deception and violent deaths, it is easy to understand how such phrases were often viewed as stupid fantasy and fell upon deaf ears.

Much of our current national press corps was growing up during that era. Others in the media, who were already of age, simply sold out or went with the flow as factual reporting was phased out to make way for dollar driven infotainment... or at least they didn't put up much of a fight. Whatever the combination, and while the what-if's and if-only's are endless, there is no question that today's news thrives on the sensational... and those who interpret it shun fairness for the sake of a story, rush to judgment sans conscience and damn-the-consequences, and greet any truth but their own with disbelieving smirks and/or wholesale distrust.

For years, every time there was a TV story about Bobby or Dr. King or JFK, my children would ask, "Are you going to cry, Mom?" Often, I was too choked up to answer. But then I was mourning the past. Today, I mourn for the present. For generations who, courtesy of the sneering, rancorous media, seem to know zilch about people who can instill a sense of possibility and/or social commitment... except, to link their names with revolving scandals about babes and boobs and beds. And no, I am not mourning for a society whose leader is less than perfect. Kennedy was no saint. Neither was FDR nor Dwight Eisenhower nor Thomas Jefferson. Etc. I do mourn, however, for a society whose gross national product has evolved into hate mongering and back fence gossip, and whose gross national conscience promotes vicious cynicism.

It does not have to be this way. No matter how entrenched or historically bad the media's track record, We the People can fight back: turn off and tune out hate radio and tabloid TV. Quit reading all the 'gotcha garbage' which substitutes slander for our right to know. Boycott products whose advertising dollars encourage distortions of factual, relevant, unbiased dissemination of the news.

We also have the right to demand accountability. Yes, after years of relentless pursuit, President Clinton literally got caught with his pants down. And he lied about it, too. But, back to page one, there was more than enough guilt and outrageous behavior to go around. Within hours after 'Lewinskygate' broke—when it was still nothing more than unsubstantiated rumors—Sam Donaldson predicted Clinton's resignation by the coming weekend; yet the President's approval ratings soared. The next week on *60 Minutes,* still wallowing in unproved allegations, a sneering Andy Rooney belittled Clinton's lifelong Sunday church attendance as a photo-op. Common decency aside, where else can highly paid representatives of vast multi-national companies draw conclusions strictly from gossip and/or make totally out of touch projections and still keep their jobs?

At that juncture, neither Donaldson nor Rooney nor any reporter could know for sure if Bill Clinton was guilty of anything. What was clear however, was that for every small fact, there was a ton of unadulterated, salacious supposition. What was equally clear was that the pundits were hell-bent on humiliating the president. Smugly and self righteously denying that their interest was prurient—or money driven—they speculated, scrutinized and hypocritically passed judgment on Clinton's sex life with no restraint and unabashed glee. On prime time.

Do we truly want to become a country where, in concert with the media, a zealot like Ken Starr makes the rules and criticizing him equates to treason… or at least to being dragged before a Grand Jury? Do we really want to be a country where friends are expected to tape friends and betray their confidences? Or an entire presidency is defined and undermined by a relentless 40-million-dollar investigation which finally uncovers foolish indiscretion at best, or, at worst, sex between two consenting adults? Ratings be damned! Greater issues than sales and Neilsens are at stake here. Are headlines really worth the rape of the Bill of Rights?

The media savaged President Clinton's 'denying the effects of his actions;' yet they continuously deny responsibility for the effects of their own actions—and words. When members of the press behave like a bunch of hormone raging adolescents, disregarding fairness and destroying truth for shock value, we'd all benefit if their mouths could be washed out with soap. I, for one, would be delighted to hand them the bar. A money driven, vengeful, sex-obsessed press nearly paralyzed the Clinton Presidency and jeopardized my, and every citizen's, Constitutional guarantees. It is up to We the People to preserve and protect those guarantees… and to tell the press (1) to grow up and (2) *no more!*

✍

1 San Francisco Chronicle, July 10, 1994

2. Ibid.

3. CNN—Attorney Karen Smith

4. San Francisco Chronicle, August 16, 1994

III

Special Circumstances

The Gift of Travel

Open Up Those Hearts and Minds... and Be Sure to Pack Your Manners

The old world village of Glastonbury is the New Age capital of England. On this site, according to legend, King Arthur once reigned and Merlin performed his magic. Today—in perfect covenant with its mystical past—Glastonbury's narrow, winding alleyways abound with fortune tellers, astrologers and occult book stores run by sandaled proprietors wearing headbands.

Legend also has it that Arthur and Queen Guinevere were buried in the local abbey. Their bodies mysteriously disappeared when Henry VIII ordered the abbey's destruction in 1539. Yet, as if in defiance, a sense of majesty still reigns among its ruins. Wild flowers sprout inside the crumbling archways and the royal gravesite—marked only by a plain, wooden sign—lies on grounds so peaceful that one feels transported across centuries and connected to all who have come before.

Filled with this spirit, my husband and I sat drinking tea in a local shop. And a guy from New York barged in complaining at the top of his lungs, "There's nothing to do in this damn town! Why did the bus stop here anyway?"

Another time. Another trip. "Paris is two thousand years old... " the guide began. Although his words came as no surprise, I felt overwhelmed just being there... until a flat, mid-western accent shattered my reverie. "No wonder this place looks so old and dirty! Why don't they tear it down and modernize it?" Within the same three-hour tour, the woman also complained about menus not in English and scoffed at the Eiffel Tower, saying, "No big deal. I like the arch in St. Louis better.'

What motivates people to spend a small fortune visiting places they have no interest in? What compels them to deride everything they see as too old, too small, too strange, too boring or simply not good enough? What makes them treat differences in language and culture with ill concealed contempt or behave in ways they'd never dream of back home? And why do I care?

When a Portland couple wanted to sleep-in at our hotel near Munich, they ordered the concierge to tell the local church not to ring its bells. It is a safe bet they would never have acted that way visiting Disneyland. In the improbable event they did, however, it is also a safe bet I would find their request preposterous, but not personally embarrassing. Yet why is it, that whenever I am overseas and fellow Americans behave as if their manners were jettisoned over the Atlantic, I feel like crawling underneath the nearest table?

For better or for worse, identity is powerful. Total strangers can bask in each other's accomplishments solely because of some common heritage or tie. Ex-pats around the world seek out compatriots. Tourists burst into animated conversations with strangers who speak the same language. When the unmistakable voice of Vin Scully declared via Armed Forces Radio, "It's a beautiful afternoon for baseball in California... " never mind that my husband and I were having a marvelous time in Germany. Never mind that Scully broadcast the Dodgers and we are Giants' fans. Suddenly, we both felt homesick.

Identity is our bond with the world as we know it... and foreign travel disconnects us from all things familiar. The customs are different. The currency is different. The language is different; or if it is not, the same words can mean something else. It is easy to feel displaced and disoriented, and thus joined at the hip with anything 'back home.'

While that may address the personal side, what about the embarrassing? If we dismiss the unpalatable tourist as a jerk acting in character, or graciously concede that folks sometimes handle new situations with fear and upset, and even if we decide none of it has a thing to do with us, the icky feeling remains. Why? It comes back to identity: if we can feel linked to strangers' achievements, we feel linked to their offenses as well. That, and a bit of the Marge Schott syndrome where colleagues cringe not only because of what has been said, but because they believe it reflects badly on them.

Yet tourist-based guilt by association is not a wholly self-centered reaction. Nor is it entirely self imposed. Pigeonholing people *en masse* because of the actions of a few is a routine, often destructive, human habit. While the results may be relatively benign where tourists are concerned, they are no less distasteful... especially if the 'few' are very vocal, very rude or otherwise attention grabbing. One British tour guide blithely told a group which included fourteen U.S. citizens, "The only thing Americans are even interested in is *where is the ice machine or the bar?*" While she may have been misinformed, kidding or was simply not thinking, her statement clearly reinforced two truths: (1) Stereotyping seems inherent to the human condition. And (2) A tourist's worst traits become the benchmark by which his/her compatriots are judged.

This same guide declared May 8, 1945 was "V.E. Day—Victory for the Empire," so I could not put too much stock in her perceptions. In both instances, Americans deserve more credit... although I admit that regarding the ice machine, my exasperation was more personal than patriotic. I simply do not wish to be classified among the bozos.

Nor do I want them to rain on my parade. Each time I am a tourist, I want to fall in love with the experience. I want thrill to the adventure, bask in the pleasure and learn as much as I can... because I consider the opportunity to travel among the greatest gifts of my life. The gift did not come early. Nor has it come easy. Since neither of us was born with a 'silver spoon,' my husband and I have juggled finances, family matters, work schedules and all sorts of priorities to make our trips possible. And we have been incredibly lucky.

Business has taken him overseas, and courtesy of the aforementioned juggling act, he has taken me. We have also had some terrific vacations. We've known the joy of spending weeks at a time in other countries... and the location of all the bargain restaurants. We've had the sometimes funny, sometimes frustrating experience of being two professional communicators reduced to plaintive smiles and ersatz sign language. We have soaked up the history, thrilled to the culture, been awestruck at the sights, called at birthplaces and graves of the great, climbed ancient stairways to the tops of castles and cathedrals, kissed the Blarney Stone and visited memorials that capture the pain of war's appalling losses.

We've learned the world is very small. In the men's room of the Sheraton Hotel at Frankfurt Airport, my husband met a fellow member of our community chorus back home. Both guys were so stunned they couldn't remember each other's name, never mind that they both sang baritone. In the Tower of London where Anne Boleyn, Sir Walter Raleigh and countless others met their inglorious end, I ran smack into a colleague with whom I'd shared an office in San Jose. We stared at one another for a few seconds before exchanging shrieks and hugs. Since the Bloody Tower is well known for its history of beheadings, shrieks were probably once pretty routine there. On the other hand, a new chapter may have been written with the hugs.

If traveling reveals how small the world is, it also reinforces how round... and how tied it is to the circle of life. It is an incredible feeling to see where journeys began and where they ended, and understand the impact that they had. To have visited Plymouth, Massachusetts where the pilgrims landed, and then to visit the Pilgrim Steps in Plimouth, England and see where the Mayflower was launched. To have toured Robert Louis Stevenson's home in Monterey, California, then see his birthplace in Edinburgh. To have attended umpteen Shakespeare festivals, including Stratford, Connecticut's, then to visit Stratford-on-Avon and tour the homes where Shakespeare was born, grew up, wrote and lived with his wife Anne Hathaway. To have experienced the Beatles, then visit the Beatles Experience in Liverpool. To pay homage at Chopin's grave at Père Lachais Cemetery in Paris, and discover fresh flowers are placed there daily courtesy of the Chopin Society of Bartlesville, Oklahoma.

Yet keeping an open mind is the requisite traveling companion. That, and allowing the nourishment of one's imagination, is as important as carrying a passport... because how we receive the gift of travel is all in the perception. There was that cold, windy day in Ireland for example, when we watched a master craftsman thatch a three-hundred year old house. One could view that as a chance to learn about a very special art, or wonder why stand there freezing just to see some guy fix the roof on an old dump. Hadrian's Wall, built—depending on who is telling it—to keep the Romans out or the Scots in, or Stonehenge, or the crumbling ruins of Germany's feudal castles can either be seen as marvels of history or a bunch of old rocks. Mass at Notre Dame is arguably the best free organ concert in the world. But rather than experience its majesty, one could easily say, 'I never go to church and besides, I'm not Catholic.' Sainte Chappelle could be dismissed as 'glass is glass.' The Bonnie Banks of Loch Lomond as 'water is water.' And munching Cornish pasties on the shores of the English Channel could always be compared unfavorably with hot dogs at the ball game.

Keeping an open mind allows one's appreciation to roam far and wide and deep. Yet there are always tourists who mistrust uncharted territory or thrive on being negative. Others apparently get more of a thrill telling folks where they've been than from actually having been there. Still others never leave home without their American Express cards but forget to pack their imaginations. In every case, that is their prerogative. As long as they allow me the privilege of enjoying what I enjoy as well, so be it... although I cannot help but feel it is a shame to close out the world at large.

It also seems a waste to let minor inconveniences interfere with adventure, excitement and feeling memories. When we visited the poet's Wordsworth's grave in England's Lake Country, the day was cold and wet and icy rain dripped down our necks. Rain also dripped off the canopy and down our necks at an outdoor restaurant in Paris and drenched us when the wind blew our umbrellas inside out at Père-Lachais. We wouldn't have missed any of those adventures, any more than I would have missed eating haggis in Scotland, even though my ankles swelled like crazy as a result.

Then there was the time we couldn't find the gas-cap release on our rented car, and the instruction manual was in German. We also got lost driving in the Austrian Alps. Yet we finally found Salzburg, a city of incredible beauty resting under the watchful eye of the oldest remaining fortress in Central Europe. We explored the fortress. We also visited Mozart's birthplace and saw the clavier on which he composed. And, at a concert in the Dom, Salzburg's landmark cathedral, we heard the organ on which he practiced.

If the Dom and its environs looked familiar, that was because it was easy to visualize Julie Andrews and her Von Trapp youngsters dancing through the town square. In fact, one day when it rained so hard no one dared to venture out of the pension, our hostess ran *Sound of Music* on the VCR... and the hills were alive with the sound off-key music as a gang of stranded tourists identified local landmarks and turned the video into a sing along.

Living near San Francisco, we are used to seeing familiar sights in movies and on TV, but that doesn't take away the fun of incorporating literary and/or cinematic sightseeing into our travels. In the cold-war spy flick, *Hopscotch,* run-away CIA agent Walter Matthau receives a note from the KGB while he's hiding out in Salzburg. The note reads, "The fountain... eleven AM." We located the fountain in the gardens of Schloss Mirabelle and made sure we were there at eleven. In London, we saw the Changing of the Guard, Big Ben and Westminster Abbey. We also made a point of visiting 221B Baker Street, now the Sherlock Holmes Museum, and of looking for 84 Charing Cross Road in honor of its literary and feature film namesake. Initially, we were startled to find the shop which once housed a book store specializing in rare first editions was now a Pizza Hut. But, happily, it turned out we were wrong. Number 84 was empty and looked much the same as it did at the movie's end. Pizza Hut was across the street.

Throughout the British Isles, I half expected to see the sisters Dashwood or Eustasia Vie running across the fields or Miss Marple peeking around the corner. Later that year, we were able to re-experience Wales through *The Englishman...*" Ireland through *Circle of Friends,* and the Scottish highlands through *Rob Roy.* And since the last time we saw Paris, every TV show, commercial and news clip filmed there spurs wonderful memories and a longing to get back A.S.A.P.

I grew up dreaming about Paris. It may be known as The City of Light, but I knew it as the city of Gene Kelly and Leslie Caron. It would be more than thirty years after they danced along the Seine before this American got there, but it was worth the wait. While we didn't duplicate the dance, we did sing the Kingston Trio's *The Seine* outside of Saint Germain des Prés and as "We walked along the river till dawn was coming nigh."

I'll leave the travelogues to Michelin and Fodor's; except to agree that Paris is radiant, magnificent and definitely a city for walking. Aside from the pickpocket who outwitted us on the crowded Number 1 Metro Line, it also has efficient, inexpensive, user-friendly public transportation which we rode all over the place during our weeks-long stays there.

In 1989, we were lucky enough to be in Paris for the bicentennial celebration. On the eve of Bastille Day, we picnicked on the banks of the Seine and watched fireworks over the Eiffel Tower. The next night, we watched as Heads of State from around the world gathered to join the festivities at Place de la Concorde. Two centuries earlier, on the very same spot, crowds also gathered and cheered... as the guillotine dispatched more than 1300 heads, including those of Marie Antoinette and Louis XVI. Visiting there can be thrilling or chilling, depending on one's mood.

Dickens' *A Tale of Two Cities* defines Paris of that era as, "It was the best of times, it was the worst of times." Though happily times have changed, it is still a city of contradictions. From *hâute couture* to flea markets. From *hâute cuisine* to MacDonalds. From the Louvre to the guy who sketches tourists for as many francs as they are willing to pay. Standing near the tip of the Ile de la Cité, one can look west to see an awe-inspiring, gothic tribute to the magnificence of human accomplishment, the Cathedral Notre Dame. From the same spot, one can also look east and see an inescapable reminder of human brutality: a memorial to the 200,000 who were deported to—and died in—Nazi concentration camps.

On a smaller, but no less profound scale, such remembrances are all over Paris. Plaques on schools and apartment houses commemorate the children and adults who were dragged out and sent away. Plaques also recall those who died "Pour Là France." I knew the Liberation troops had entered the city at Port d'Orleans. I also knew Port d'Orleans was the last stop on the #4 Metro. Wondering if there was a memorial to Marshall LeClerc, I rode the subway to the end of the line and discovered a typical bustling neighborhood with apartment houses, parks, shops and restaurants... and sidewalks filled with plaques memorializing where one young person after another died during the liberation. *Morte pour Là France. Aôut 1944.* There is also a cemetery within walking distance of the metro. This is not a resting place of the famous where guides conduct walking tours. This is a quiet, simple cemetery is filled with quiet, simple graves adorned with miniature flags. Etched in each stone is the final story of too many young lives. *Ages 17, 18, 19, 20. Morte pour Là France, August 1944.*

Yet during the fiftieth anniversary of D-Day celebrations, a well known American news anchor postured in front of the Arc de Triomphe and spoke of Paris as having been liberated "without a shot being fired." How convenient to rewrite history if it makes a better story. How quickly the world forgets. And precisely because such memories are discarded, young lives will continue to become memorials etched in stone and pain.

The aftermath of war is evident wherever we have traveled. Wars long past. Wars in the conscious memories of many of the living. Public wars. Private wars. Political wars. Royal wars. Wars fought in the name of the religion. In Edinburgh, we visited the chapel where Mary, Queen of Scots, once placed her five-day-old son in a basket and lowered him the equivalent of about fifty stories. Servants then spirited the infant away to be baptized as a Catholic. Religious wars were quite serious in those days... and it does not seem as if the world has learned a lot since. In time, by the way, Mary's child, James IV of Scotland became James I of England. His mother didn't fare nearly so well. She was beheaded at the command of her cousin Elizabeth I, daughter of Henry VIII.

Commemorating a very different, more modern, but no less bloody time: in Coventry, England, we visited the cathedral dedicated to peace which stands adjacent to the ruins of the cathedral destroyed in the bombings of November, 1940. Remembering the same war, but on the other side of the world, we visited the famous guns of Fortress Singapore which were pointed in the wrong direction. Singaporeans smilingly point out that their main World War II memorial resembles a giant, granite chopstick. And sadly, in spite of today's thriving, modern city-state, many still recount the Occupation as if it happened yesterday.

War memorials also dot the German landscape. I admit to having been startled—and even offended—when I first encountered plaques and statues dedicated to those who died for the Fatherland, 1939 to 1945... until I allowed myself to think about what I was seeing. Commemorating the foot soldier, I realized, does not pay homage to the people who create wars. Nor does it endorse monstrous policies. Shrines such as these are meant to honor and remember the sons, the brothers, the husbands, the fathers, the friends and the loved ones who, because they were young and male and of a certain nationality at a certain time, ended up losing their lives. Remembering the dead is a separate issue from victory or the judgment of history. Besides, if the only battles and martyrs any country memorialized were from wars which were won, Americans would have no Civil War sites in the South, and no Vietnam Wall.

It was a profound lesson. Opening up our hearts and minds enriches our wisdom. It allows us to re-evaluate preconceived notions. It also enables us to make peace with a past that cannot be changed, appreciate the present that is, and to better understand that all of it is part of a great, ever-evolving, ever-unfolding panorama.

I can think of no greater example of this than the year we spent Christmas in Munich. Once the cradle of the Third Reich, this beautiful, friendly city is now known as the Christmas capital of Bavaria. Every December, the country's top artisans, craftspeople and musicians gather to display breathtaking decorations and hawk their wares at *Christkindlemarkt,* a delightful Christmas street faire.

Christkindlemarkt is a happy, festive, freezing month-long celebration... warmed up considerably by steaming cider and mulled wine. I shopped for everyone on my gift list at the faire and spent long hours gazing at other bargains I could not afford. On December 24, my husband and I headed downtown to enjoy the end of *Christkindlemarkt* and ended up shedding quite a few tears and one more pre-conceived notion. Expecting to witness German efficiency and see everything quickly dismantled after the noontime closing, we found instead that, in a laid-back spirit of the season, booths are simply boarded up and not pulled down until after New Years.

We also found a joyous gathering at Marienplatz, the square in front of city hall. I am not certain if 500 or 5,000 people were standing there bundled against the cold, although it probably was somewhere in between. We joined them to watch a charming closing ceremony topped off by lederhosen-clad musicians playing Alpine Christmas Carols from a balcony overlooking the square. The mood was enchanting. The music exquisite... if not very traditional for us *auslanders.* Then came the final carol, as familiar as holly and Santa Claus and blessings of peace.

Stille Nacht. Heilege Nacht. The notes rang clear in the chill December air. Silent Night. Holy Night. And as often happens with well-known melodies at Christmas, everyone began to sing. We joined the chorus—in English—and from across the square we could other's singing in English with accents different from our own. We also heard the sweet sound of French. Lilting notes in Italian and Spanish. Unfamiliar words of more than one Slavic origin. *Stille Nacht. Heilege Nacht.* Silent Night. Holy Night. A harmony of words. A melody divided by language, yet together in verse, sound and celebration.

And there, for one shining moment, was not only our greatest Christmas gift, but the greatest gift of all our travels. Through the common bond of music we witnessed the ability of people to cross imaginary borders with good will as their only passport. It was the voice of humankind united. United in a prayer for peace.

✍

No Experience More Overwhelming

A Pilgrimage to Dachau

I stare transfixed at the picture in the newspaper. It is of a blue-eyed, blond-haired little girl. Feature for feature, she looks so much like my own childhood pictures, I feel as if I am seeing a mirror across time. Even our long curls are worn in the same Alice-in-Wonderland style. But she is not me. Her name was Anny-Yolande Horowitz. The photo is from her identity papers, issued in 1940 by the collaborationist Vichy regime. Two years later, when I was skipping off to kindergarten in my native Providence, Rhode Island, Anny-Yolande was deported to Auschwitz from her native Strasbourg, France. She was gassed upon arrival.

Today, pictures of my childhood and growing up fill our family album, along with photos of my own babies and their growing up. And Anny-Yolande's face graces the cover of a memorial album containing photographs of 1500 French children... just a sampling the 11,000 who were shipped to Nazi concentration camps.[1]

When I look the picture so similar to a little girl that once was me, I can imagine the feelings of a San Francisco woman who visited the Holocaust Museum in Washington, D.C. Her maiden name was Eva Heymann, and she was born in Berlin on the 13th of February. Handed a folded, commemorative card inscribed with the name and birthday of a victim, Eva opened it to read, *Eva Heyman, February 13.*[2]

These stories represent more than chilling coincidence. They are examples of how the fabric of all lives is interchangeable, and its patterns determined by fate, luck or time and place. Any person's tragedy could just as easily belong to another.

This lesson is intensely magnified when one retraces the footsteps of those who perished. Visit a restored concentration camp, and the dead once walked on the very paths which you now follow. They wore the tattered uniforms now displayed behind protective glass, perhaps on the very spot where you stand. They entered the same buildings... including the *Krematorium* which they exited in ashes. You feel their spiritual presence and can almost hear their cries. No commemorative cards are necessary. The entire experience is in memoriam.

It rained the day we went to Dachau. We drove through the magnificent Bavarian countryside, my husband and I, observing that the dark, somber sky seemed an appropriate backdrop for our pilgrimage. We also sadly marveled at how such horror could spring from a place so naturally beautiful... or that a country so rich in its history of the arts and scientific accomplishment had been capable of such barbarism. Our conversation was sincere and well-intended, yet it soon seemed like empty intellectualizing. Realizations are swift inside a former concentration camp. One: illusory backdrops are neither appropriate nor relevant. The sun never truly shines on places of horror. Two: the only answer to incomprehensible 'hows or whys' is that human evil exists—even in the midst of accomplishment and beauty.

We drove into a parking lot adjacent to the camp. A group of high school students was exiting a tour bus and, like teenagers everywhere, they were jostling and joking. Their leader issued a stern reminder that this was hallowed ground. I was to cross paths with the group throughout the morning. The admonition had not been necessary, for not even exuberant youth can ease feelings that envelop the body and soul when one enters the gates of Dachau. Like all other visitors, the students made their way in hunched-shouldered, overwhelmed silence.

We had followed the young tourists as they walked from the parking lot. Many opened brightly colored umbrellas against the rain. At the sight of the stone wall pock-marked from bullets and the towers which once housed the SS guards, those colors seemed to fade from existence. Recollections of that day remain monochromatic. Stark. Bleak. Black on White.

A structure which once warehoused victim's confiscated possessions and where gruel intended to starve the prisoners was brewed, has been converted into a museum. It is now filled with artifacts and precise records, and photograph upon photograph of children and adults… freezing, frightened skeletal remains of human civilization. I cannot recall the building's layout, but I will always remember the photographs. The eyes. Imploring. Beseeching. Entreating. Sending the message across time: Never Forget.

A long, wide gravel path leads away from the museum. One can feel—if not hear—echoes of jackboots as the tiny stones crunch beneath your feet. Row upon row of barracks once stood on either side of that path. One—possibly two—of them has been fully restored. In place of all the others is a seemingly endless expanse of bare foundations. Each represents a structure which housed imprisoned, tortured souls.

The crematorium is further down the path, the final solution to the final solution. This building, this chimney, once worked day and night to destroy the evidence of lives destroyed. The sight of it—the reality of it—assaults the senses. So does the ironic, twisted message above what was once the camp's main entry gate… *"Arbeit Macht Frei,"* the cruel hoax which translates to, "Work Makes You Free." Each of my legs felt as though it weighed five hundred pounds as I walked through there. My God! What must it have been like to pass through—one way—as a prisoner?

Nothing is masked at Dachau. No punches are pulled. No excuses made. No better example of a nation's atonement exists than in the restoration of this concentration camp. Facing truth at all costs, the unthinkable is laid bare and every visitor consigned to a descent into hell. I was too overwhelmed to think that day, and for a long time afterwards. Only with the passage of time I was able to recapture the magnitude of the experience… in verse:

We walked where they walked,
but not in their footsteps.

We stood where they stood,
but not in their shoes.
There were moments
when our eyes locked.
There was
no other way to communicate.
The swelling
in each of our throats was too great.
The pain, too profound.
There can be no experience more overwhelming,
than standing
on this hallowed, horrifying ground.

In the museum,
there are once-worn garments
of prison stripes and imprisoned pain.
And pages upon pages
of documents.
Meticulously kept records
of human beings turned first to numbers,
then to ashes.
There are photographs of children
reaching out across the generations with imploring eyes.
And I wondered, not entirely without foundation,
If one of them might be a distant cousin.

I am not certain
if that is when it started.
I recall only realizing
that sounds were forming
in the innermost reaches of my head.
Words I no longer know,
from decades long past.
Words I could not repeat today were I asked...
And yet they took shape.
Became louder.
More clear.

Until I understood I was hearing,
then silently repeating.
Repeating.
The Hebrew prayer for the dead.

We can pray for the dead. But what do we say to them? What do we say to Anny-Yolande Horowitz and Eva Heyman and all the others? How can we give life to their legacy of *Never Forget?* Or ensure that our inherited responsibility of *Never Again* remains more than a convenient, contritely-worded phrase? How do we make good on that watchword of the survivors and the penitent vow of a world community who stood by, but did not see?

We can begin by telling the truth. We can stop pretending that what happened was an aberration or a frenzied, historical accident. We can look at Dachau, Auschwitz and all places like them and admit that genocide was neither born there nor did it die there. It long predated Hitler's concentration camps... and continues now. Today's haunted eyes may stare from the face of a Catholic or Protestant mourner in Northern Ireland, an ethnic Albanian or a Bosnian Muslim or a Rwandan caught up in ancient tribal warfare. Yet, is the human tragedy less meaningful? The eyes also stare from children caught up in a world which offers them no hope. Are the young whose lives are cut short in American ghettos today any less dead than those dragged from the Warsaw ghetto in 1942?

Secondly, we can acknowledge that scapegoating—and the need to blame any one group *en masse* for all the pain, tragedy, humiliation and ills of the world—is itself a root cause of much of the pain, tragedy, humiliation and ills of the world. Ethnic hatreds, religious persecution, racism and tribal rivalry thrive on wholesale condemnation and are made worse when passed from generation to generation. No matter what atrocities have gone before, there is no justification for blaming the yet-to-be-born.

Ancestral crimes are not blood debts owed by their descendants. Nor should the innocent be held accountable... although doing so makes it easy to justify one's own hatreds and dishonorable behavior. "I was ostracized," recalls the daughter of German immigrants of her girlhood in 1950's America. "I was teased and ridiculed at school... I had stones thrown at me and was spat upon." Surely this child, conceived a year after Hitler blew himself up in his bunker, no more helped to create the Third Reich then little Anny-Yolande posed a threat to her own native France. Yet, like countless others who were either not born or far too young to endorse Hitler's psychotic world, this German-born child was made to endure pain—and guilt— for 'the sins of the fathers.'

Forty years later, she described her own recent pilgrimage to Dachau, confiding, "Intellectually, I understood I was not responsible for the atrocities, but emotionally I could not shake the shame for the horror my native country had participated in... In order to be internally reconciled, I somehow needed to be in the presence of the tortured souls of the past. To offer my own hurting soul in order to cleanse and restore myself."

How unjust that this woman felt forced to atone for brutality of a previous generation. Yes, her despair at humankind's capacity for evil was wholly appropriate. And yes, it is understandable that, as a German-born American, she would mourn her birth-country's history. And certainly as a citizen of the world, her personal commitment against future atrocities should have been a given... but because it was the right thing to, not because she is an inheritor of shame or accountable for anyone else's past.

A forebear's crimes are part of no one's DNA. Neither is the drive to retaliate for an ancestor's victimization. That is a cultural obsession taught and learned. One which keeps old hatreds alive while young victims die, and renders impotent the noble concept of *Never Again.*

Never Again is a commitment to life. To the future. It is not about resuscitating the past. Nor is it the about avenging the dead. In fact, the two are contradictions in terms; for, unless the past is laid to rest, battles—and vendettas—and killing—and genocide will continue to span the decades and the centuries and the millenniums. And what will be accomplished? No act of the present can bring back the dead, even past odds or succeed in changing history.

Serbs annihilating Muslims cannot annul what took place in

the thirteen hundreds. Planting a bomb in Paddington Station will never reverse the outcome of the Battle of Derry. Being a survivor of—or the child of a victim of—the Holocaust does not entitle present-day Israelis to become the butchers of the Gaza. Neither do the agendas of Arab terrorists justify blowing up busses on the streets of Jerusalem. Nor anywhere else. And, while the United States forever bears the stain of legalized slavery, radical leaders who blame those born after the fact serve only to prevent healing, promote racism and perpetuate the tragedy. Ironically, ethnic hatred is the one thing which does not discriminate. From time immemorial, it has cursed the entire world.

If we could accept that ancestral crimes should not be inherited, then perhaps we could also eliminate their congenital legacies of Victim Olympics. Human anguish is not a contest. It cannot be compared or measured. No race, religion or nation has an historical lock on agony and life offers no gold medals for grief and torment. Accordingly, nothing positive will ever be gained from images of genealogical groups shouting, "We suffered most... We're Number One" and their descendants claiming, "My people have suffered more than yours... therefore, I am entitled to make you suffer, too!"

Since the living cannot settle the scores of the dead, then perhaps instead of concentrating on righting past wrongs, we should pay homage to what messages the departed might have for us. If they could rise from their graves, would our ancestors call for revenge and further violence, or would they tell us that history is a fact which cannot be rewritten and the future something we owe to every child? I would rather imagine the latter. Just as I would rather believe that if those whose presence I felt at Dachau could rise from the ashes, they would join with those who were incinerated at Hiroshima, and those who died shackled on slave ships, and those who died in wars, and all other forebears whose lives ended in violence and tragedy... And they would send the world a clear, single-minded prayer: *Remember, but do not blame the innocent. Learn from the past, but look to the future. Our message to you—our children's children—is live in peace so we can rest in peace.*

Amen.

✍

1. San Jose Mercury News, October 27, 1994

2. San Francisco Chronicle, August 30, 1994

Multiples of One

When Do They Become Important Enough to Matter?

Volumes have been written about how overwhelming tragedy numbs the senses. And how images of large scale suffering eclipse the reality of individual victims. Yet studies rarely address how massive human catastrophe is used to minimize and even disallow misfortune on a lesser scale.

The following narrative is based on events which occurred in the nineteen seventies. Perhaps some minor details no longer apply; however, the story's star-crossed lessons retain a profound—and shameful—timeliness.

A single-parent mother of three signed a long-term lease on a charming, almost-affordable home. The house was roomy and in a respectable neighborhood with good schools and convenient shopping. Mother and kids were ecstatic... until they learned that their next door neighbors were members of the American Nazi Party.

It wasn't just the swastikas, they didn't even see them at first. Instead, the family was bewildered when their windows were smashed, gas lines were tampered with on the car and harassing phone calls starting coming at all hours of the day and night. When man next-door threatened their nine-year-old with, "Fucking Jew! I'm going to throw you into the oven..." however, things began making twisted sense. And so did one woman's odd-esy of running around in circles getting nowhere.

Calls to the police resulted in her being told (1) she should pack up the kids and move, (2) she should sue, and (3) nothing could be done unless the people next door physically attacked her or her family. She was also informed that those neighbors had filed a complaint when her children's cat wandered into their house.

A visit to her attorney resulted in the woman being further informed that fear for a child's safety was no legal justification to break a lease. He also advised her the costs of a civil suit—which might enable the family to live in peace—were beyond her means. Noting that his client barely made it from paycheck to paycheck and her court-ordered child support was faithfully iffy, the lawyer instead offered to contact the Anti Defamation League on her behalf.

But the Anti Defamation League declined to get involved. There was no *proof* anyone was in danger… and, under protection of the First Amendment, the Nazis had the right to call the family any names they so desired.

A call to her rabbi resulted in the woman being referred to the Jewish Community Relations Council. They, in turn, confided that similar types of harassment occur—and often—in every major city in the United States. But maintaining a "low profile" was an unwritten 'commandment' of Jewish agencies.

The woman protested that keeping a low profile meant caving in to the haters. She also spelled out how such a policy isolates victims, makes them appear paranoid, prevents them from getting help and blocks the public from knowing the truth. The JCRC Director countered that playing down so violent a disease was the best way to prevent an epidemic.

From the vantage point of over twenty years, and in the light—or darkness—of AIDS, I wonder if he remains convinced epidemics can be prevented by denying the disease. I also question, against the backdrop of today's racial polarization and chilling resurgence of anti-Semitism, if he still espouses the same agenda.

At the time, however, he reluctantly referred the woman to an Assistant District Attorney. Someone who was "not only Jewish," the Director confided, but had "his eye on a Federal Judgeship." A game of verbal volleyball ensued. Judge 'Wannabe' implied the family's problems stemmed from having no man in the house and his legal advice consisted of, "Find yourself a husband." When the woman countered that the root cause of anti-Semitism was not unmarried females, he shot back, "You have to realize these people feel just as self-righteous in their cause as you feel in yours." "What cause?" The woman wanted to know, adding that she and her kids sought only to be left alone. Wannabe then suggested she apologize to her tormentors and promise them her family would modify its behavior. "But we are the victims!" The woman reminded him... at which time he proposed she was either concocting the story to get attention or that her family was provoking its own harassment. His final recommendations included (1) see a psychiatrist, and (2) submit the case to arbitration.

So it was back to the Jewish Community Relations Council... whose contracted attorneys vetoed the idea of arbitration. There was no guarantee the referee wouldn't be anti-Semitic, they cautioned, hence the woman could be denying herself Due Process. Conceding that litigation was still her best—and perhaps only—alternative, they also reiterated that a law suit was far too pricey.

"But legal expenses work both ways," the woman countered. "Once my neighbors understand how much a law suit could cost them, and especially if I appear to have JCRC backing, they might decide the aggravation isn't worth the money." She then suggested a 'cut it out or I'll sue you' letter... making it clear she would gladly pay the lawyers for their time. And again the attorneys demurred. Since they had no authorization to undertake a lawsuit, they were in no position to write such a letter.

A system which does not respond to its victims gives immeasurable power to their abusers. The harassment continued. Sometimes it was threatening and potentially dangerous. Other times it was the incessant, exasperating life-interrupting type designed to drive its targets nuts... like when the Nazis attempted to file criminal charges because a volleyball accidentally sailed over the fence. They also reported the woman to the police for "going up and down the street shouting anti-Christian epithets." Astounded, the accused told officers responding to *that* call that they were looking at a clear case of projection. Yet the irony and satire were not lost on her. "To recoin a old phrase," she added. "Some of my best friends are going to be very surprised."

But it was no joke. The police disclosed that Mrs. Nazi was keeping a log of the family's comings and goings. Included were the physical descriptions, license plate numbers and exact arrival and departure times of all guests… who the peeper was demanding be investigated. "But people go in and out of *their* house wearing swastikas," protested one of the family's teenagers. Expressing neither surprise nor doubt at that revelation, the officers then told the woman and her kids, "Strictly between us, you are dealing with the worst kind of nuts."

Once again, the police voiced concern for the family's safety. Once again, they urged the woman to obtain legal counsel. Once again, she tried to follow their advice and the JCRC attorneys said legal help was too expensive, either on a private basis or for the organization they represented. These attorneys were likewise indifferent when, later on, the family was served with an illegal notice of eviction… even after the woman personally questioned the landlords, and they confirmed the Nazis had berated and threatened them for renting to Jews. The landlords also assured the woman that the ouster was nothing personal. They just did not want any trouble.

Eviction on the basis of religion is against the law, a JCRC attorney reluctantly agreed, after being maddeningly incommunicado for nearly two weeks; nevertheless, the case was still too costly to bother with. Even if moving would cause severe financial hardship, he further noted, illegal eviction did not make the landlords responsible for the family's expenses. Before he hung up, he did advise that the woman find the money to move somehow and be glad she was getting free of her lease… otherwise the landlord could sue her. She also remembers with bitterness that he wished her luck in her new home.

I know the JCRC thinks I am a pain in the ass, her diary from that time reads, *but I see this as both a Civil Rights issue and an example for my children. A home is a basic right. I want my kids to know no one should be denied that right because of their religion…*

The woman's diary may have been simpler and less eloquent, but how different were her feelings then from what Dr. King secretly wrote in his *Letter From A Birmingham Jail?*

> *"When you suddenly find your... speech stammering as you seek to explain to your six-year-old daughter why she can't go to an amusement park that has just been advertised on television... and see her begin to distort her little personality by unconsciously developing a bitterness toward white people; when you have to concoct an answer for a five-year old son asking in agonizing pathos: Daddy why do white people treat colored people so mean?... then you will understand why we find it so difficult to wait."*

When she had to concoct answers for a nine-year-old being threatened with incineration and teenagers told they had to move because of ancestral ties or where they did or did not worship, then one can understand why she couldn't agree to just quietly move.

HUD was sympathetic; however, the landlords owned only two pieces of property and they (HUD) could only get involved if there were four units or more. The Human Rights Commission was also sympathetic, but they were hampered by the same restrictions.

Somewhere in this time frame the woman's esoteric feelings about basic rights gave way to disillusion and practical cynicism. It dawned on her that the legal system is about money not justice, that laws are often unenforceable and meaningless, that the agencies designed and funded to help people can range between indifferent and impotent... and she was totally on her own.

But as she became more pragmatic, she also became more determined. So through trial, error and tenacious research, she sought out—and found—a maverick, store-front type civil rights attorney. That the lawyer specialized in gender discrimination was a bonus; on the other hand, perhaps that is why she was brave enough to acknowledge the existence of prejudice, bold enough to challenge it, ethical enough not to base legal advice on the almighty dollar and rational enough to recognize that a woman in a vulnerable spot is not the cause of evil in the social order. And when this attorney proved her client's first instincts had been right on track, the woman wondered why she'd been dumb and/or naive enough to bother with anyone else in the first place.

For a minimal fee, the lawyer wrote one strong letter acknowledging the pressure the landlords were receiving from avowed members of the American Nazi Party. At the same time, the letter cited the 1968 Fair Housing Law and reminded the landlords they could be sued for punitive damages in Federal court. They backed down immediately. The eviction was rescinded.

It was definitely a moral victory. Whether it was also a Pyrrhic one was something only time would tell. And time proved the woman right again. Apparently the landlords were more afraid of a lawsuit than they were of the Nazis, and must have told them so. And apparently, when the Nazis thought the woman would actually fight them in court—and probably when they considered the financial consequences—the game just wasn't worth it. Whatever their reasoning, the harassment abated. In the meantime, another diary entry reads: *Some people think now that I won on principle, we should just move and have peace. Others think we should stay. Mother is worried about our safety and I worry about safety, too. Do I have the right to jeopardize the kids? Am I? But it is really not a safe world, so aren't I at least teaching them principles? On that subject, most of my friends say they admire my courage and I am an example for all. But in all honesty, all I want is a place for my kids and me to live. Hell, among my friends there's even a debate as to who are the true villains: The Nazis, or the landlords for cow-towing to their demands...*

That debate missed the mark. Beyond next-door Nazis and spineless landlords, there were equally culpable villains. Those who devised the 'low profile' policy, for example, relegating victims to the expendable pile in order to maintain an illusion. Responsibility also lay with loopholes in the law. And squarely on the shoulders of all those in a position to do something who chose, instead, to sweep this family's plight under the rug.

The Anti Defamation League knew scapegoating and harassment are basic components of racism. The Jewish Community Relations Council knew such problems were pervasive. Both agencies knew the woman's predicament was real and perhaps dangerous—threatening to throw a child into the oven leaves little doubt about the perpetrator's mindset. Making their inaction doubly disgusting is the fact that many people support—and contribute to—these organizations in the belief they are meant to help individuals like the members of this family.

And then there was Judge Wannabe. Justice is supposed to be blind. But was he blinded by sexism or ambition? Or both? In either case, he would allow nothing—including his heritage—to get in his way. So much for the integrity of the Bench.

Perhaps the decision makers who turned their backs were convinced the illusion served the purpose of a greater good. What a cop-out. People are real, not illusions. And leaving families like this to twist in the wind was—and is—an evasion of moral responsibility... one which gives life to Edmund Burke's words, "The only thing necessary for evil to triumph is for good men to do nothing." Consciously or not, when they resorted to the time-honored practice of dismissing or blaming the victim, the drop-out decision makers closed ranks with the haters. Their choice also delineates how emotional numbers rackets control societal accountability. *What was the lady complaining about anyway? It wasn't exactly Nazi Germany.*

Of course it was not Nazi Germany. In this country, racism occurs in the classroom, in housing, in the job market and in the workplace and, yes, even in middle class neighborhoods... but not in concentration camps. Does that make small-scale discrimination an inferior evil? Do victims of individual persecution actually suffer a lesser hurt than those persecuted *en masse?* Is one-on-one prejudice less destructive or less dangerous in the long run? In reality, one-on-one does not exist. It merely describes a symptom. Every riot, every race war, every lynch mob, every Holocaust begins somewhere. For every child like this family's who is threatened with a toss into the oven, hundreds of thousands actually ended up that way. Must we wait for numbers to reach such epic proportions? When does it sink in that every human being is of value? Just when does it become important enough to matter?

For one thing, it apparently matters when tied in with photo-ops and political expediency. Back when the woman was fighting daily harassment, the American Nazi Party opened a Rudolf Hess

Book Store six blocks from her home. Holocaust survivors protested in front of the building carrying signs reading "Genocide is NOT Freedom of Speech." A man who had lost much of his family in concentration camps stormed the place and gutted it. Public officials joined prominent members of the Jewish community and rushed before television cameras. Proclaiming support of the man's actions, they also passionately declared that they would never allow the city's residents to relive Nazi persecution.

Watching the scenario unfold, the woman thought, "Perhaps they'll believe me now. After all, these Nazis have to live somewhere, even if it is next door to me." But what looked good at a press conference had little to do with reality. Help was not forthcoming. Once again, this woman was hit in the face with the realization, "No greater burden can be borne by an individual than to know no one cares or understands."[1]

I am not claiming this family's circumstances were comparable to those of the man who trashed the bookstore. At the same time, neither were their experiences unrelated. Persecution is an ongoing threat. Proclaiming it as something which will never be *relived* ignores the ongoing aspect and relegates the horror to an historical accident which happened on another continent. The suffering of the Holocaust staggers the imagination; however, linking that experience only to the past turns survivors into 'they.' They… those who are apart from the rest of us, and therefore are not quite 'we.'

Yet it is enduringly 'we.' The outrages of the world do not always happen in other places and to someone else. It is both short-sighted and incredibly dangerous to think otherwise. The idea of Nazis picking on an assimilated American family was disquieting, and certainly it took less effort to blame the victim than devise a plan of action. However, I do not believe the people who refused to help this woman were blindly sexist or really considered her of inferior social value and/or not worth the bother. On the contrary, I believe her predicament scared the hell out of them, so it was easier to insist it did not exist or would go away if she did, or if she and they just ignored it.

The myth that the Holocaust had forever defused anti-

Semitism had been promoted for over thirty years at that time. Perhaps hiding behind a low-profile policy seemed preferable to admitting it did no such thing. Perhaps it was, and is still, more consoling to mouth the words "Never Again" than to accept the possibility of never say never. But 'easier' is rarely—if ever—right. Malignancies do not disappear because of wishful thinking. Neither do they confine themselves to a single target.

Nearly a decade after this woman's battle, the city where she lived dedicated a memorial to victims of the Holocaust. It was desecrated days later. While some saw the act as a warning the past could repeat itself, others brushed off those concerns as ethnic hysteria and even defended the desecration as artistic protest. It is difficult not to despair at such social blindness. Artists do not destroy in the name of art. People like the woman's next door neighbors do exist however, and their hate is capable of destroying more than memorials.

On a hopeful note, nearly another decade later, a Chicago judge ordered bigoted haters to sell their house and move away from the minority family they had harassed for nine years. On a hopeful/less-hopeful note, the neighborhood where the woman and her children once lived is now the subject of town meetings about racism and hatred. It seems the newer Asian population is being targeted by swastika-type graffiti and various hate inspired crimes. "If those who could have helped had listened to me then," the woman wonders, "would there be these problems now?" Probably yes; but there might also be some mechanisms in place to help prevent, diffuse and deal with them.

Finally, on a less-than-hopeful note, there has been an alarming resurgence of anti-Semitism in this country and around the world. "The notion that the Holocaust once and for all ended deadly conflicts between Jews and their antagonists has less substance today than most experts ever thought possible... " a 1994 Op-Ed column observed. And I find myself wondering how those experts could have been truly surprised. Weren't they listening? The editorial continued, "Over centuries, we have learned to expose the cancer of Jew hatred because it rots the foundations of freedom and democracy."[2] Yes, it does! And for the sake of the family described here, and all others who have experienced a similar outrage, and for all the newcomers with a different heritage but faced with similar hazards, that exposure cannot be strong enough. It is also about damn time.

✍

1. Arthur Stainback

2. San Francisco Chronicle, September 2, 1994

IV

Summing It Up and Tying It All Together

Evil Has Many Allies

But Its Greatest is Collaboration

The bi-weekly department meeting fell on Halloween, so management offered a catered luncheon to all who came in costume. Never underestimate the power of a free lunch. A record twenty-seven staffers hailed and broke bread with seldom seen colleagues as if they were long lost cousins.

The masquerade party actually resembled a family reunion. There was the nerd, the clown, the baby and the brat. The granny, the princess, the punk and the cat. The teeny bopper and the witch. The fairy godmother and even the God-fearing Aunt Tammy Faye, complete with a gigantic sequined cross and matching eyelashes. Beneath the costumed camaraderie, however, was a more ominous likeness to gatherings of some clans. The atmosphere was rife with discontent.

The word dysfunctional may be as hackneyed as the words abuse and denial; but this work-pretend-family was its prototype. An arbitrary management solved problems by laying blame and linked job security with catering to its blunders. Frustrated, the staff indulged in mutual fuming or simmering in silence, collective subterfuge or stabbing colleagues in the back. The result was a quagmire of unresolved issues, feigned loyalties and fundamental distrust.

Dysfunction has its roots in such basic dishonesty. No family, no workplace—no anyplace—is problem free. But denying, camouflaging or dispatching dilemmas by shooting-the-messenger only causes them to magnify and multiply. Granted, some solutions are unpleasant, even devastating. Others are elusive. And still others amount to choosing the least awful of alternatives... and no choice comes with a guarantee. Yet, repeating a message from the chapter, "It Ain't the Brady Bunch," no matter how painful or overwhelming, the best possible chance for any dilemma's outcome lies in how candidly the truth is confronted. And how honestly it is handled.

Why, then, are denial, appeasement, neutrality and pretenses of perfection more the rule than the exception? And why does 'shoot the messenger' seem like a credo of the human condition? One on one, perhaps the answer lies between fear and ego. And between the theories of two respected authors.

In *How Good Do We Have To Be?,*[1] Rabbi Harold Kushner challenges the notions, *I have to be perfect for people to love me* and/or *I have to be perfect to be worthwhile.* Recalling a congregant who'd lived in fear because of these premises, Kushner recounts how the man told of lying, making excuses and blaming others rather than ever admitting he'd done something wrong. Only when he lay dying did the man realize it was defensiveness—not his imperfections—that had turned people off. And "... that you don't have to be perfect to be worth loving. I only wish I had known that sooner."[2]

The populace of Scott Peck's *People of the Lie*[3] would be immune to any such lesson. Even on a deathbed, their egos would never allow it. Peck, too, speaks of people who lie, blame, make excuses and attack others instead of facing their own failures. Only he takes it a step further, linking them with what he terms human evil: "Because in their hearts they consider themselves above reproach, they must lash out at anyone who does reproach them. They sacrifice others to preserve their self image of perfection."[4]

Somewhere between the psyches of the self-imposed unlovable and the self-proclaimed unerring, are critical junctures: where does fear of being unworthy end and a basic lack of integrity begin? And if lack of integrity is fear driven, at what point does the fear mutate? When does its resultant 'wish to be perfect' turn into resolute worship of one's own perfection? And then, where does the dread of being unmasked as imperfect leave off, and the willingness to sacrifice others begin?

Unfortunately, those questions are not limited to first person singular. They apply to every social institution which is presumed (or presumes itself) above reproach. To every societal covenant which claims one reality and practices another. And to every situation which touts the moral high ground while it tramples in the low.

From 'loving' families who abuse and hate, to morale-spouting employers who dehumanize their employees, to a system of justice that isn't, to a free press wallowing in reckless disregard for the truth, and even to bereavement in a culture which discounts grief and loss... common humanity seems to operate from faulty major premises and by ensuring that those faults are never unveiled. Or is that too benign? Instead, for the sake of authority or appearances, does it operate through the killing power of lies and the willingness to sacrifice whatever and whoever gets in the way of maintaining them? For at what point does a faulty major premise turn into a bold faced lie? And where does a culture's dread of its lies being unmasked leave off and its willingness to sacrifice the innocent begin?

Sacrificing the innocent does not necessarily mean tossing virgins into volcanoes. It refers to anything anti-life. Anything which deliberately and/or unwaveringly sacrifices the well being of one or many in order to disguise the truth, abet a lie, settle a score, make a profit, promote a social concept, or further someone's or some entity's self interest. It is as basic as ratting on or lying about a co-worker to make brownie points with management. It is as ominous as attorneys knowingly endangering the community and even freeing killers to kill again in the name of 'protecting a client.' It is the U.S. Supreme Court declaring that subsequent proof of innocence is no reason to overturn a conviction so long as the guiltless party received a fair trial. It is the physicians' conspiracy of silence in the face of a colleague's negligence or glaring malpractice.

Also included is the betrayal of a sibling to usurp an inheritance or gain family favor. But not included is the harboring of a sibling felon or covering up any relative's crimes. Recalling "Ritual Torture," families can also have conspiracies of silence... and even dub them codes of honor. But blood ties or not, any code that endangers innocent victims is not honorable.

When David Kaczynski found compelling reasons to suspect his brother Ted was the Unabomber, he agonized, sought expert advice, tried to shield his mother and refused any possible reward. Then he did the only decent thing. Yet while law enforcement and much of the public applauded his courage, the media initially had a field day dissecting his character. Headlines screamed 'What Kind of Man Turns In His Own Brother?' *Time* even wondered if he hadn't been motivated by a bit of revenge or some childhood jealousy. Excuse me? Common ancestry does not cancel one's responsibility to the common good. Of course David's decision was infinitely more painful than had the suspect been his co-worker or the guy next door. The question, however, was never 'what kind of man would inform on his brother,' but 'what kind of man would not turn in a possible serial killer?'

"Easter Week..." claims the phrase 'media ethics' is oxymoronic; and one more time, their issue here was sales and Neilsens... not integrity. Nor was their sub-issue truly DNA. It is doubtful that the press would have been so enamored with the bonds of biology had David kept mum in the name of brotherhood while Ted continued to blow people up. In fact, it's a safe bet they'd have demanded the brothers Kaczynski share a cell. In the meantime, the words 'his own brother' echoed over and over, sometimes emphasizing *own,* other times, *brother.* And at all times implying that—regardless of circumstance and/or the costs in human terms—filial bonds demand absolute, unconditional loyalty and anyone who breaks the mold is a rat fink.

The profit-driven zeal to devaluate David Kaczynski did not come about in a vacuum, however. Once again, it simply capitalized on and pandered to one of our culture's most resolute myths... "the dangerous, unexamined belief... the family is a microcosm of an ideal world."[5] Imperfect people and dysfunctional families date back to Genesis, hence the ideal-myth is clearly a fairy tale. It is also a puzzlement. It shouldn't take a rocket scientist to understand that, since families are comprised of human beings—good, bad, strong, weak, honest, dishonest and even decent and/or indecent—they can no more symbolize a perfect world than can the world itself. Acknowledging filial frailties (fairly, honestly and sans hidden agendas) does not equate with disloyalty. On the contrary, it is an act of love—for it frees a family to confront the challenges which need confronting.

Unfortunately, while some families face a loved one's failings head on, others blame phantoms or bury their collective heads in the sand. "No one in our family would get involved with drugs unless they were influenced by someone else," an acquaintance defended her grown son's cocaine addiction. Another despaired over her daughter's manic depression with, "These kind of things just don't happen in my family!"

Yes they do. Mine. Yours. Hers. Bad things not only happen to good people, they happen to good families—and not always to someone else. Neither do bad families always happen to somebody else. Perfectly nice people can have emotionally disturbed or cruel, or even evil, relatives. Some have the courage to recognize illness and/or malevolence among their kin—and respond accordingly. Others, like the family in the following narrative, become poster children for the connection between filial and societal dysfunctions.

The well documented story of 'Jessa B.' is neither fictional nor, on the surface, unusual. In public, she was all charm and grace. In private, she waged war on her family's souls. Yet while Jessa's version of wife-and-motherhood bore greater likeness to a meat cleaver than a June Cleaver, her behavior is not what makes this story germane. It is her family's long term response to it.

When her children were young, Jessa beat them unmercifully and threw tantrums, fits, knives and hot frying pans. Then, she would ridicule the kids' bruises, accuse them of being clumsy and joke with friends and neighbors about having tomboys who always seemed black-and-blue. *Ad infinitum.*

The woman's spouses fared little better. Her children grew up witnessing such scenes as their mother attacking Daddy from behind, pouring boiling coffee down his back, and then accusing him of scalding *her.* Decades later, one week before her bed-ridden, eighty-six-year-old second husband died, Jessa dumped the man's urinal over his face... then called for protection as a battered wife.

While Jessa's capacity for cruelty seemed beyond imagination, an adult child recalls, "No matter what happened, you never, *never* told what went on inside the house. In fact, both our parents warned—and even threatened—us that 'betraying' the family was the ultimate sin." Another grown child adds, "Dad was often outraged at her behavior; but he acted helpless in the face of it. So the result was everyone protecting our mother's image at the cost of our own safety."

Under the guise of being taught about loyalty and privacy then, responsibility for the family's welfare was sidestepped by the parents, dumped onto the kids and Jessa's children had their first lesson in sacrificing the innocent. Themselves.

Such predicaments are common to dysfunctional households. Of course no family wants its personal business broadcast all over the neighborhood; but in clans like Jessa's, the value and propriety of keeping quiet on the outside bastardizes into denying, neglecting and perpetuating what's happening inside. If no one else knows about a dangerous, abusive situation, it doesn't exist. So children learn another life lesson... the power of covering up.

They also learn the power of the lie. Cover-ups are built upon and thrive on lies. And the bigger a lie, the more it stuns its listeners; and the more it stuns its listeners, the more they believe it must be true, despite all evidence to the contrary. Since lying keeps people off balance and causes them to doubt their sanity, one daughter recalls the end result in Jessa's family being, "The only thing worse than our mother's physical attacks was her ability to twist and distort. You recognize a bruise when you see one, but her lies paralyzed you. Made it impossible to think. Even when you knew the truth, it was hard to figure out what was real."

When Jessa's children grew up and thus too old to slam, she slandered them instead. She wildly accused one or another of incest, extortion, abuse of their own children and whatever atrocity popped into her mind. Since they knew that she maligned anyone who dared to challenge her or who she perceived as a threat, none of this should have come as a surprise. But reflecting a common human failing, each son or daughter had a hard time accepting that she'd extend such enmity to *them.*

Yet why? Vilification was not only Jessa's standard *modus operandi,* where her adult children were concerned, it was also wholly logical. Not only had they the temerity to have outgrown her control, they knew that she knew that they had the goods on her. They also knew that she knew that they knew she'd 'annulled' her divorce from their now dead father, feigned being a widow whose first marriage was perfect and was now cruelly haranguing husband number two for failing that ideal. The only possible way for Jessa to prevent exposure and protect her image was for her to destroy anyone who might spill the beans. What choice did she have?

And Jessa protected her image with consummate skill. Should any grown child challenge her, she'd recoil in self-righteous horror and laughingly taunt, "I can say anything I want because no one believes a mother makes up such things." Likewise, she'd scorn corroborating evidence and demand the apostate be committed to psychiatric care. Then, publicly lamenting such disloyalty and ingratitude, she would bulldoze all boundaries and seize upon life's true problems to justify her contentions.

Even tragedies were not exempt. When a teenage grandchild was diagnosed as schizophrenic, Jessa vowed to his mother, "I'll see you in Hell before anyone calls my grandson crazy." She then tried persuading the boy to forgo treatment, 'confessed' to his therapist that her daughter had always hated and tortured this son and, against both his doctor's and mother's orders, further sabotaged the grandson's recovery by sneaking him money to spend on street drugs.

When a son-in-law was caught in an affair, Jessa not only encouraged him, she derided his wife's upset as proof that that daughter was selfish and hysterical. When the law caught up with an ex-son-in-law, a dead-beat dad, Jessa consoled him that her daughter was bloodthirsty to expect him to support his children. Ironically, both the strayer and non-payer, once appalled by their mother-in-law's behavior, now became her good friends. Of course. Finding a collective scapegoat is the essence of an unholy alliance.

So is joining forces to condone respectively unacceptable actions.

Jessa was masterful at forming such unions. She was also a master of divide and conquer, knowing in her bones that turning people one against another would take the heat off her. But why did she do this? What was the pay-off? All families have problems and not all of them are solvable, yet wouldn't it have been easier to try to live in peace and afford everyone else the same opportunity? In an ideal world, perhaps. But people like Jessa thrive on chaos. Consequently, just as "the family is a microcosm of an ideal world" is a misrepresentation, so too is the belief that peace is a universal goal.

Then perhaps more significant than the question of why did she do it, are the questions of how and why she got away with it. Her family knew she was an emotional pyromaniac who treated her kin as kindling. At one time or another, each had labeled her insane or evil or impossible. Yet long years after her children were of age, some of them continued to tolerate her abuse... if not always toward themselves, at least toward everyone else.

As far as *how* Jessa got away with it, theirs was the ultimate cover-up culture. Even normal boundaries and independence were somehow twisted into unmasking mama... and her secrets had to be kept at any cost. Fear, too, was a pervasive agenda. Fear that elevated the 'I have to be perfect to be lovable' hoax to 'not only do I have to be perfect to be worth loving, my family's matriarch has to appear perfect for people to love me, too.' Consequently, instead of standing united against her, some bore false witness against themselves and/or one another by turning a blind eye to her brutal meddling or providing a listening ear to her slander. They also catered to her tyranny by making excuses for it or, perhaps even worse, declaring themselves neutral in the face of it.

Agreed, taking sides can be viewed as childish in filial matters while neutrality is often touted as the high moral ground. But refusing to take a stand can just as easily reflect cowardice and hypocrisy. Think Swiss bankers and the spoils of war. In that case, just as whenever it is clear who is the victim and who is the villain, remaining neutral becomes morally indefensible.

That distinction should have been obvious within Jessa's clan.

As should have the difference between family spats and a filial holocaust. Should have, yes. But the yoke of afflicted kinship can sabotage both clarity and moral imperatives; thus we have the ingredients for *why:* (1) Unhealthy parent-child bonds often bequeath crippling guilt, feelings of powerlessness and the need for love at any price… and love-starved, guilty people just-as-often follow their pain. (2) Accepting betrayal from one whose love is supposed to be inevitable is among the cruelest of human tasks… and some will do anything to avoid such an awful truth and/or hide from their heartache. And (3) victims of abuse often identify with and even emulate their oppressors because they equate such behavior with power.

There is also a remarkable human need to believe in absolutes. Absolutes are comforting. Easy. They make rigid rules and allow no room for the responsibility of independent thought. They also allow no room for human complexity and variation; thus (1) can be false to begin with and (2) perpetuate stereotypes and injustice. *All* Jews… *All* blacks… *All* men… Women or children *never* falsely accuse… In Jessa's case, her, "I can say anything I want because no one believes a mother makes up such things…" metamorphosed from a conveniently created false absolute of 'mothers *never* lie.' And those who accepted that hubris rendered themselves incapable to jettison the woman's self-serving PR—or BS.

One's background and circumstances may influence who a person is, but we are ultimately responsible for who we become. So, in the long run, *how* and *why* boiled down to choice via strength of character. At the same time, Jessa's perpetual lies threw all she touched into a tizzy and created an atmosphere of collective doubt where nobody knew what to believe and nobody trusted anybody. In *People of the Lie,* Scott Peck spells out how "lies confuse."[6] and how "the evil are 'the people of the lie'."[7] This woman could easily have been his centerfold.

She could also have inspired a well known ghetto legend: two men were asked if they had a last request before facing the Czar's firing squad. When one said, "I'd like a cigarette," the other cautioned, "Abe, don't make trouble!" Since standing up to Jessa ensured one's status as a sitting duck, her children learned young that the only way to dodge her bullets was 'don't make trouble.'

And some kept right on dodging in lieu of growing up. For whether Jessa was truly evil or not, she was definitely an impossible person made possible by her family's confusion, dodging and deflecting-of-the-truth. The worst insult one sibling could hurl at another was, "You're just like mother," yet the same hurlers flocked to Jessa's house for birthdays and holidays and openly castigated and/or shunned any sib who challenged the woman or who, for sanity's sake, went missing from her life.

The family plot was analogous to, when in the face of compelling evidence, an incest victim is scorned into silence to protect the perpetrator's image. Their scenario also paralleled certain aftereffects from earthquakes, fires and floods. Original disasters do one type of damage, people's behavior in the fallout can do another. Ordinarily law-abiding citizens who turn into looters, for instance, betray their own humanity no matter how they rationalize their actions.

Jessa's enablers became masters at such rationalizing—and at betraying their own humanity. Perhaps they were in thrall to her. Perhaps they were simply too pained to accept that, yes, she really was *that bad.* Perhaps their reasoning reflected the French proverb, *Honi soit que mal y pense*—evil be to he who evil thinks—convinced that to admit Jessa's perfidy would indeed make them *just like mother.* If that were the case, they would have been better off quoting H.L. Mencken: "It is a sin to believe evil of others, but it is seldom a mistake."

If Jessa's kin seem star-crossed and dysfunctional, they certainly are not an aberration. Many, many families likewise excuse and enable their worst offenders... with similar ruinous results. And chillingly, such kindred scenarios also parallel the world at large. For how different is the coercion of one's relatives into secrecy than from the plight of a corporate whistle blower? How different is the willingness of family members to sacrifice one another than from the behavior of a whistler's colleagues?

How different was Jessa's arrogance that she could lie with

impunity than from tobacco CEOs swearing under Congressional oath that nicotine is not addictive? How different is the same CEOs' burying multiple damning reports (along with tobacco's victims) from Jessa's conniving to protect her image? How different was slandering those who might expose a family member's lies from California's spending over 1.1 million taxpayer dollars to discredit employees who'd charged sexual harassment against members of the State Assembly... even after the women's claims were validated through independent investigation? And how different was Jessa's sabotaging her mentally ill grandson's treatment from politicos who capitalize on human tragedy to further their ambitions? The Willie Horton ads. The '96 video that employed—without permission—the image of slain Polly Klass to label a campaign opponent "soft on crime."

Each variance may be a matter of refinement. Or degree. Or of dollars. But in reality, it is all the same—and the list and comparisons are endless. How different was the accommodation of Jessa's family to her emotional tyranny than are the countless historic appeasements which have resulted in tragedies and wars? Again it is a matter of degree. The question is what can be done about it?

If anything can be done, and that's a very big if, perhaps we can begin by telling the truth. Or more to the point, with telling it like it is. Many ideas that people espouse and the choices they make do not reflect what they really believe. Instead, they reflect absolutes they feel duty-bound, compelled to, or powerless not to protect. And such improvident protection—*my country, my company, my family right or wrong*—is often invalid, out-of-date and even dangerous.

Sometimes it becomes necessary to take a long, hard look at a culture's insistence that its personal, civil, financial, religious and societal premises cannot be questioned... that they are infallible regardless of their costs in human terms. Sometimes it becomes necessary to take a long, hard look at the lengths to which a family or a culture will go to preserve and protect those illusions. Circumstances shift. Traditions and schools of thought prove unworkable. Mistakes in judgment are made. Betrayal happens. Sometimes rethinking and/or changes of direction are necessary; even directions once presumed immutable or cast in stone. In this context, telling the truth has nothing to do with revealing what is no one else's business or holding one's privacy up to public scrutiny. It means facing the pain of disillusion and having the integrity to issue course corrections and the courage to tear apart myths and lies woven into the fabric of the human condition.

Telling the truth also means breaking free from absolutes and the fallacies of false premise. Yet considering how goofy and off-on-tangents we humans can be, perhaps 'the whole truth and nothing but' is a frightening and overwhelming prospect. In an atmosphere rife with political correctness, total honesty could hold such inherent dangers as revoking civilities like *How are you?—I'm fine.* After all, rarely are greeters truly interested in a litany of a greetee's troubles and, more often than not, a greetee feels no duty to provide one.

May we all be granted the wisdom to know the difference... and the ability to employ common sense. Any equivocation whose intent is to 'above all do no harm' is not in opposition with a culture based on truth. But family structures, social concepts or rules of law which sacrifice the innocent mock and defy integrity and are never, ever honest.

Nor are they ever harmless. Evil does not dwell only within far-off people and places. It can manifest itself among those we love—even our parents or our children. It can manifest itself within our culture, our nation's schoolyards, our government institutions or as part of our social order. For if it were otherwise, all families and social orders would be unfailingly humane and non-exploitive... and never has that happened in recorded history. I doubt prehistoric times were any better. So perhaps humankind's best bet lies in the honest nurturing of one's own mental health and the courage to act accordingly. Scott Peck observes that, "Mental health is an ongoing process of dedication to reality at all costs."[8] Just think: one on one, family to family, group to group, social structure upon social structure... how many Jessa-types could be defused by invoking that dedication? At least it would be a start.

✍

---

1. How Good Do We Have To Be. (Little, Brown 1996) (Parade, September 8, 1996)

2. Ibid.

3. People of the Lie. (Touchstone Books/Simon & Schuster, Inc. 1983)

4. Ibid

5. Shot in the Heart. Mikel Gilmore

6. People of the Lie. Page 66

7. Ibid.

8. The Road Less Traveled. (Simon & Schuster, Inc. 1978)